COLOR

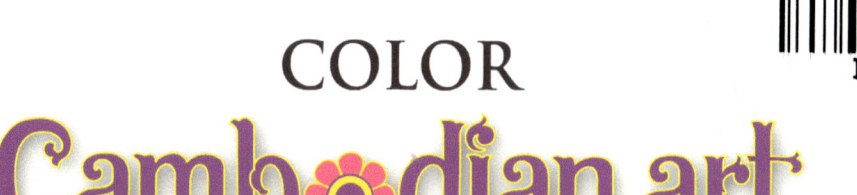
Cambodian art

I0467346

Conceived, Designed, and Illustrated by:

Mrinal Mitra

Series Edited by:

Swarna Mitra & **Malika Mitra**

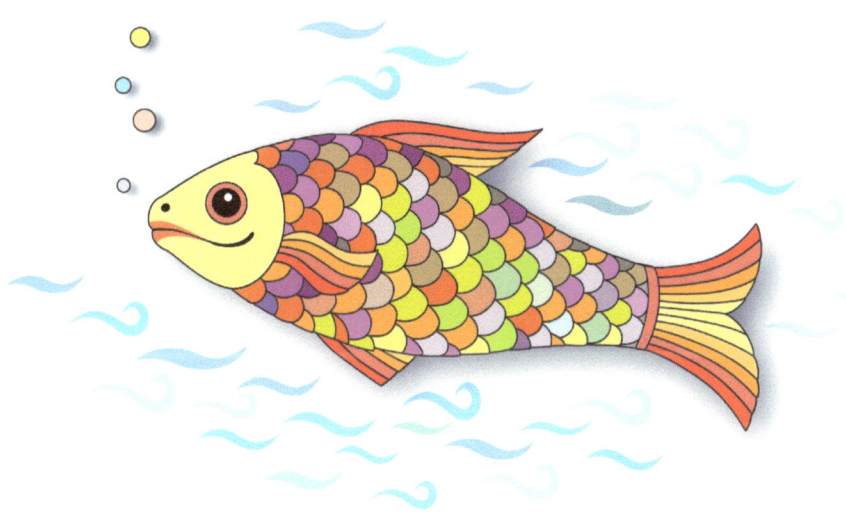

WORLD CULTURE COLORING SERIES

*This series is dedicated to the citizens of the world;
from the young blooming minds of children, to the aspired individuals of all ages.*

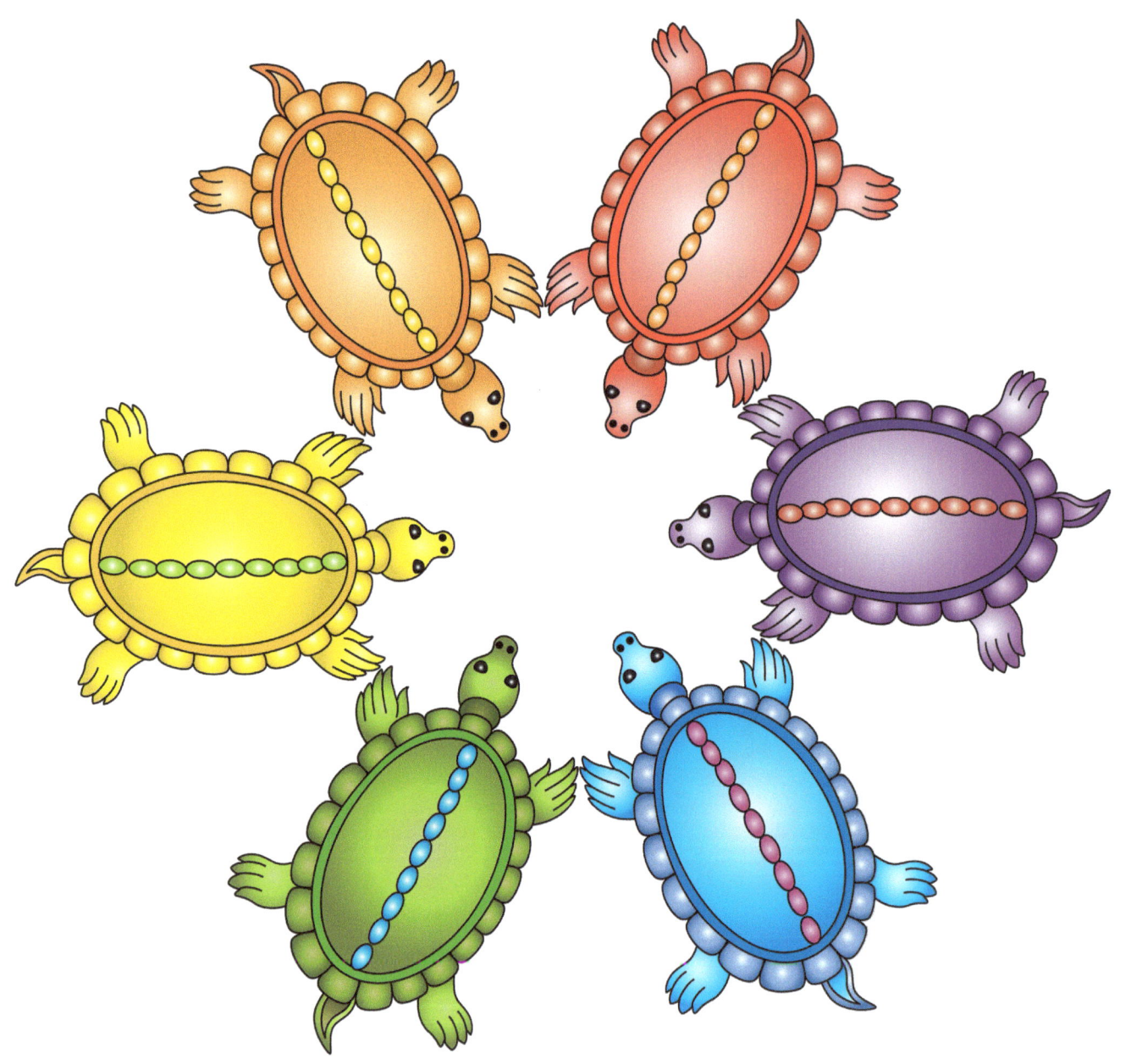

Turtles on bas-relief, Banteay Srei, Angkor Wat.

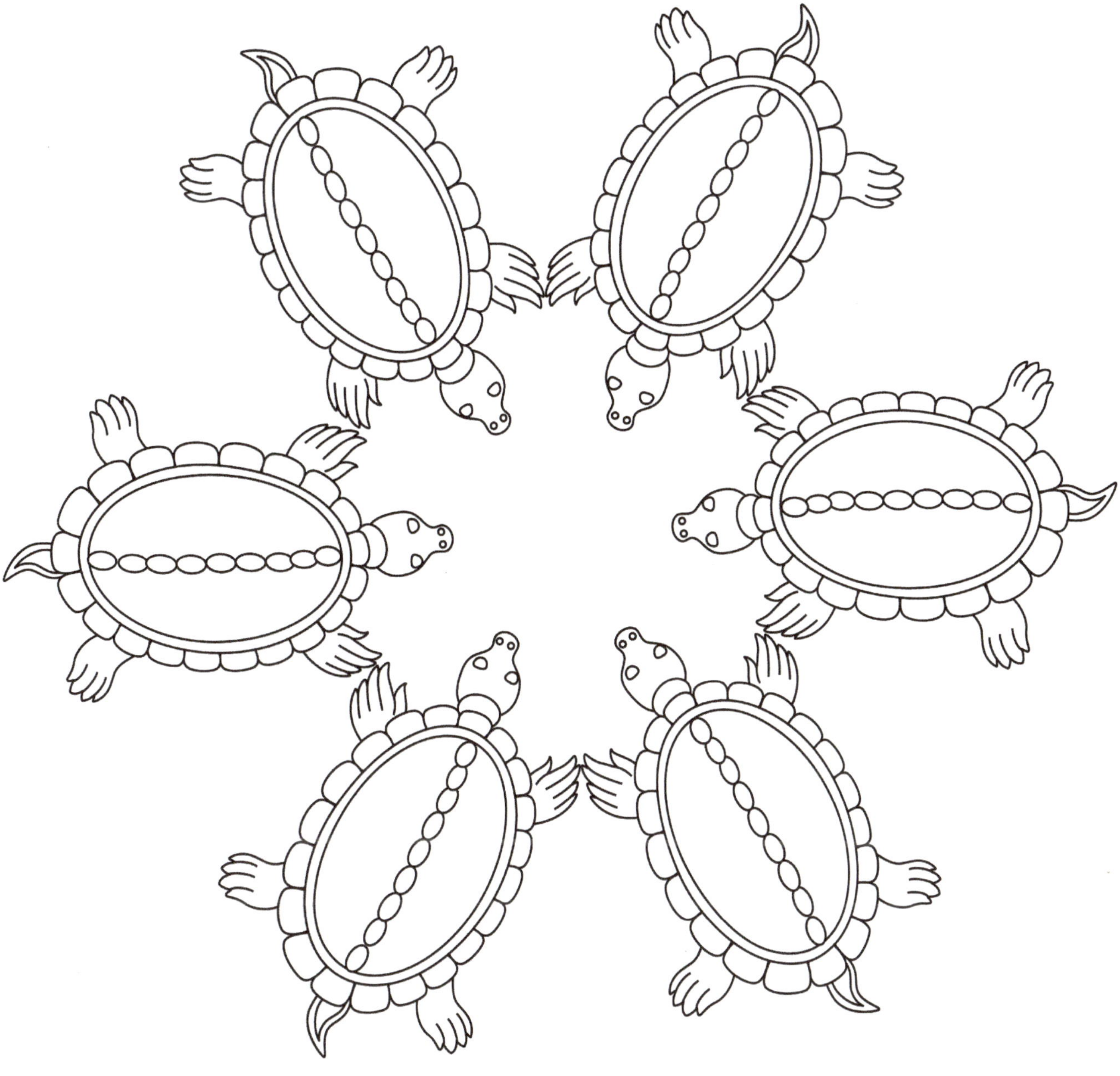

Color the drawings above using your preferred choice of colors.

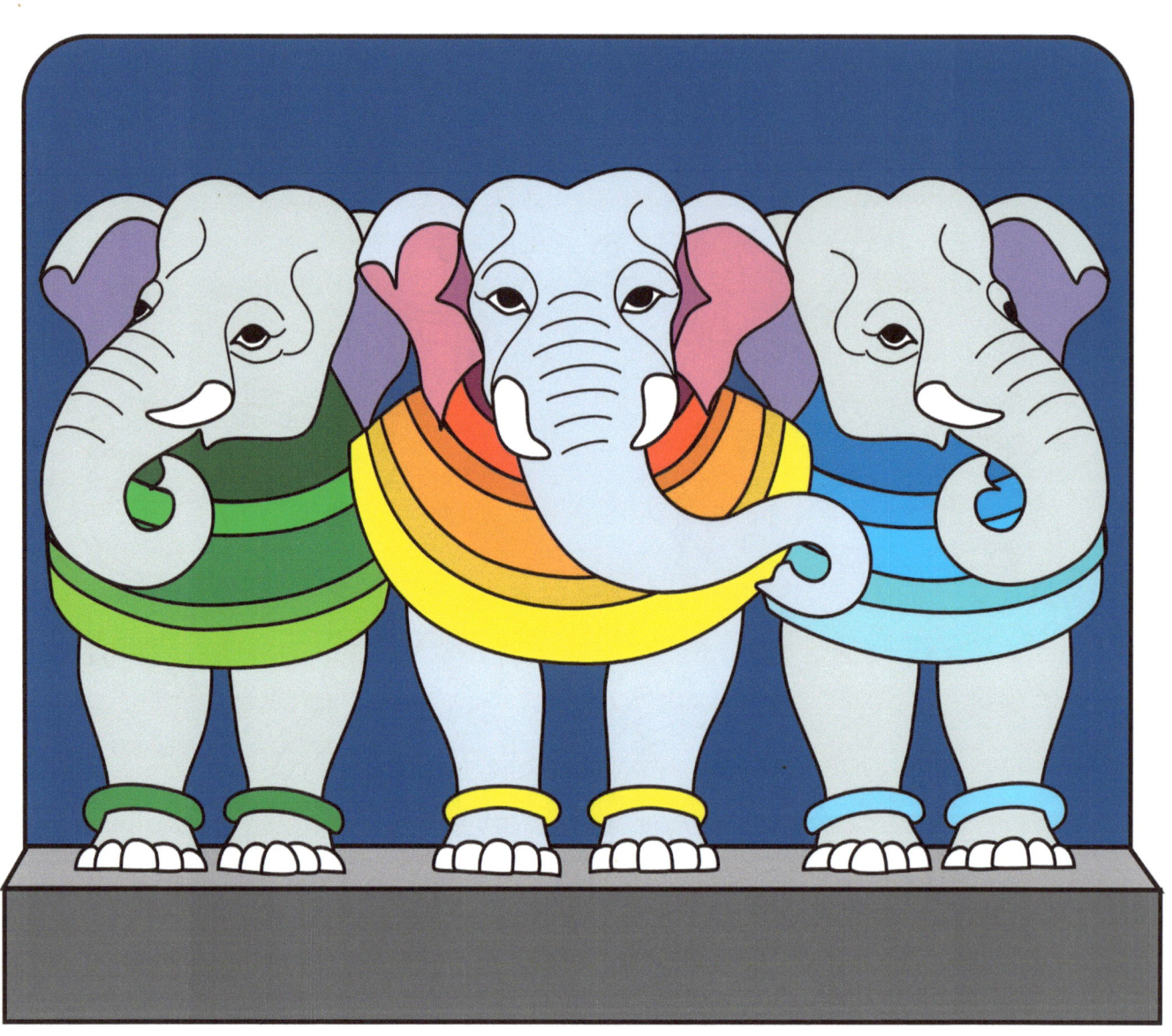

Three elephants, from a bas-relief, first pediment, Vishnu temple. Banteay Srei, Angkor Wat.

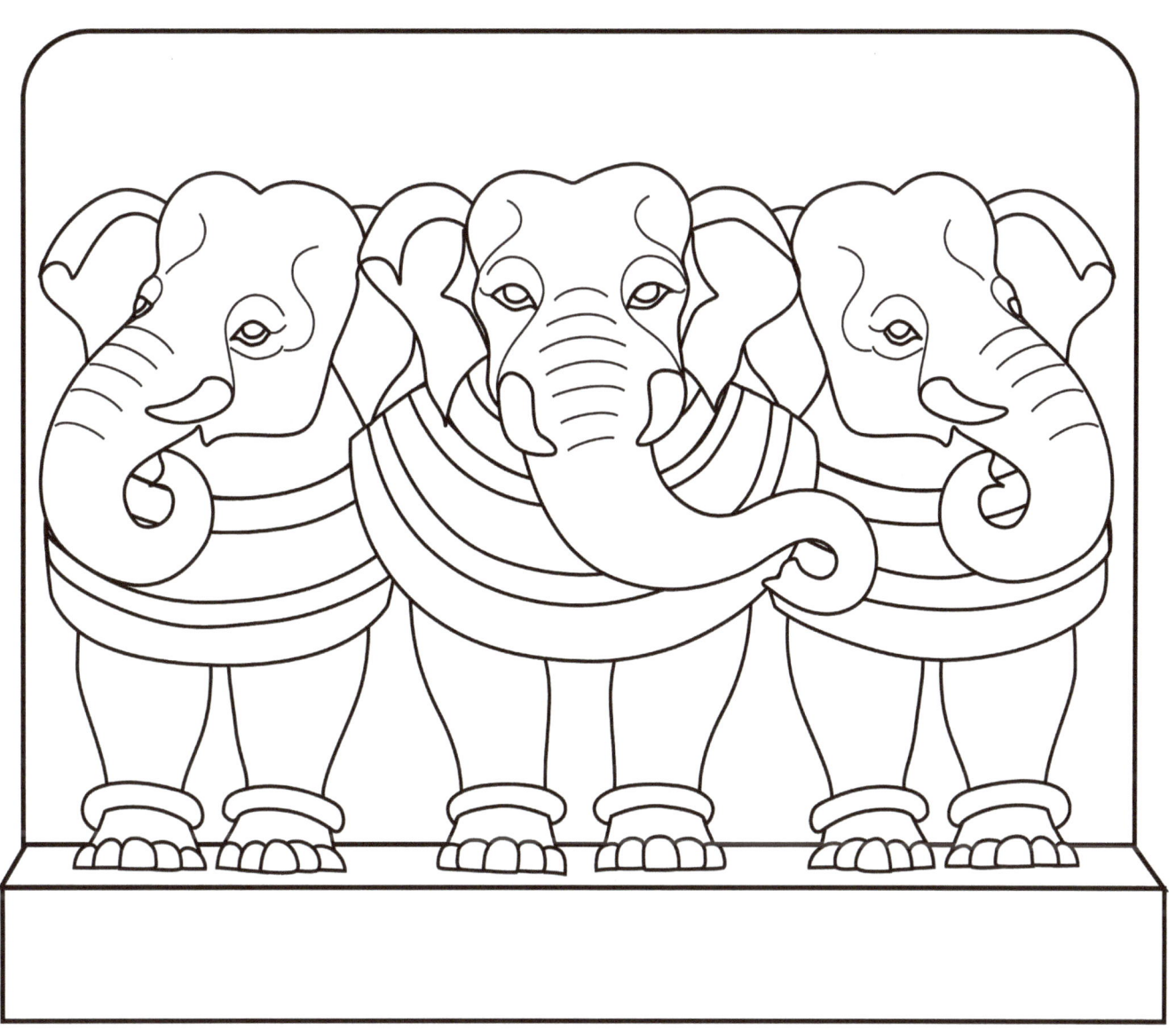

Color the drawing above using your preferred choice of colors.

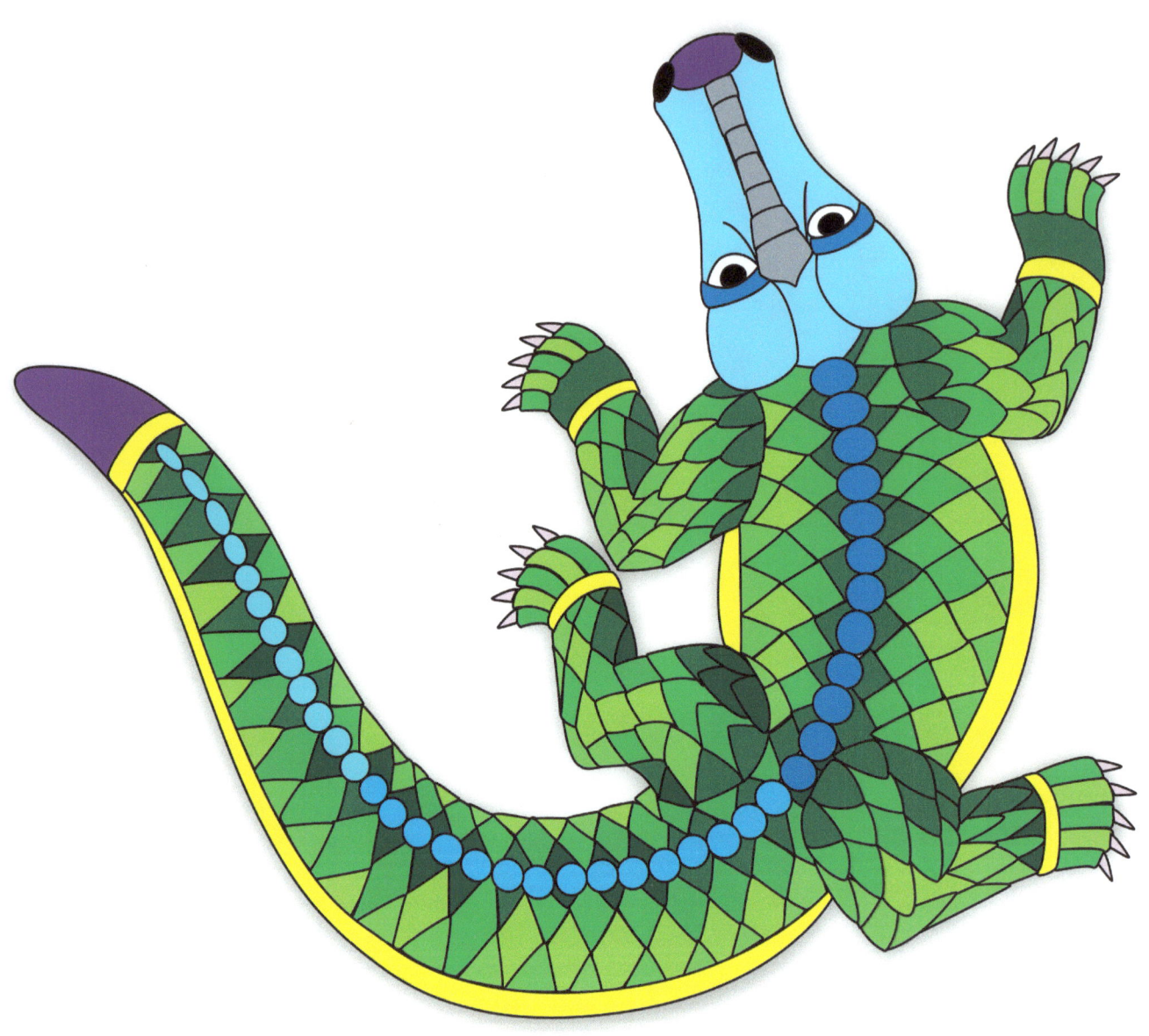

A crocodile, from a bas-relief in the outer gallery of the temple at Angkor Thom (first half of 13th Century C.E.).

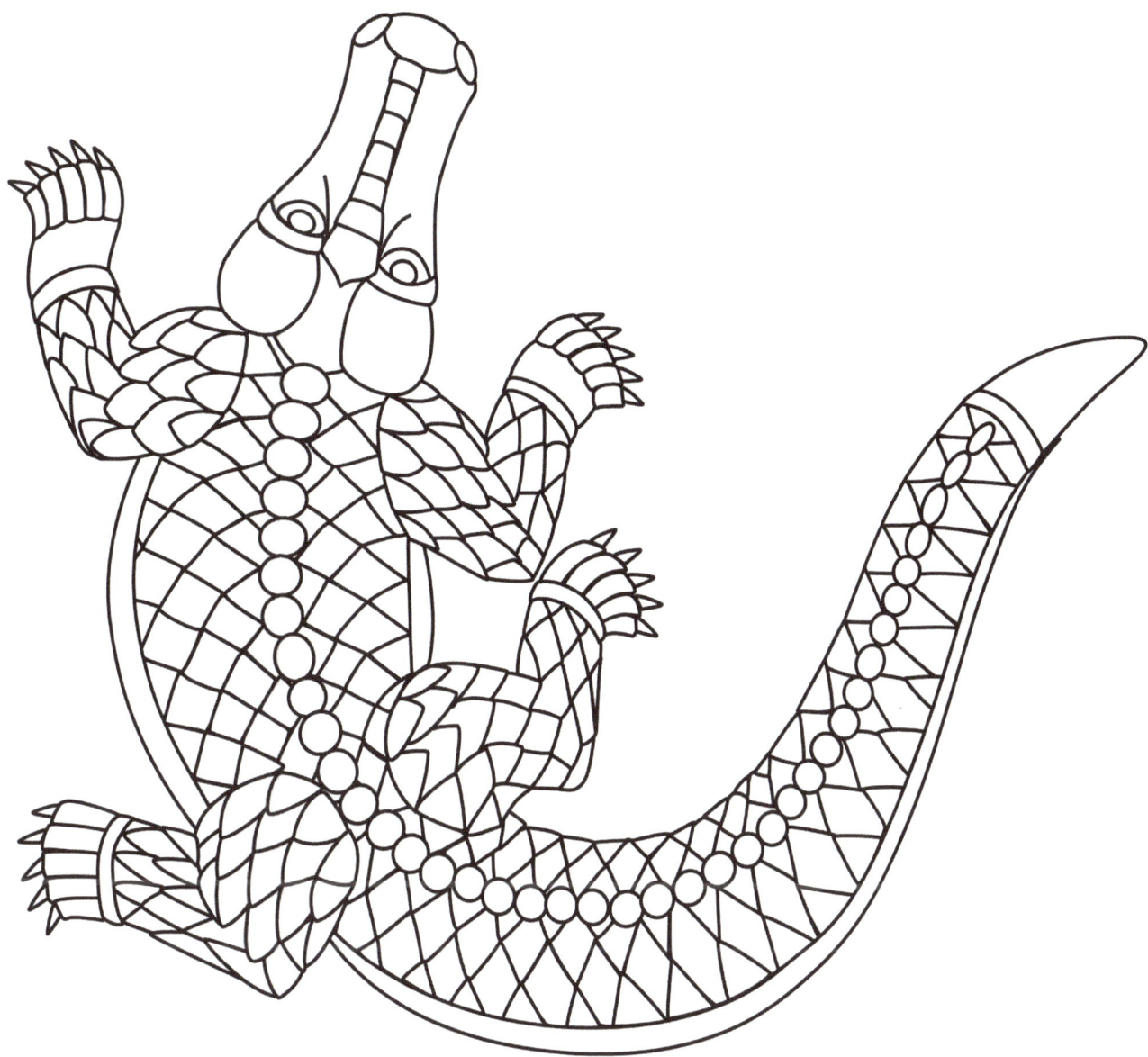

Color the drawing above using your preferred choice of colors.

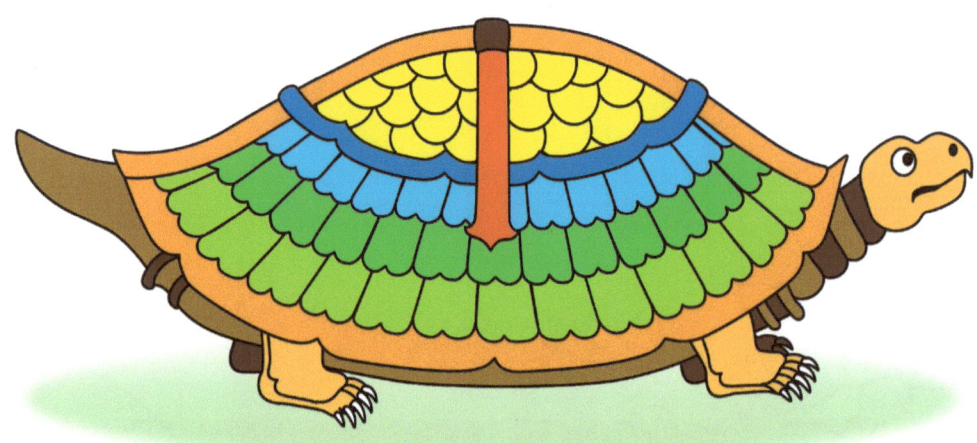

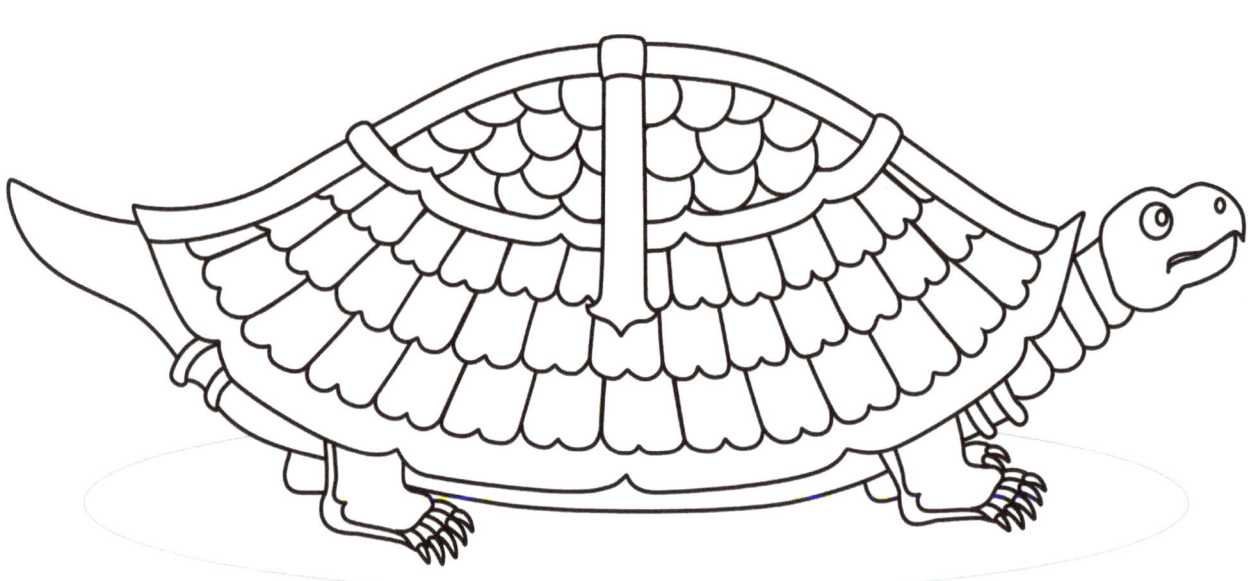

Kurma, the tortoise from a mythological scene in the relief work. The Bayon, Angkor Thom.

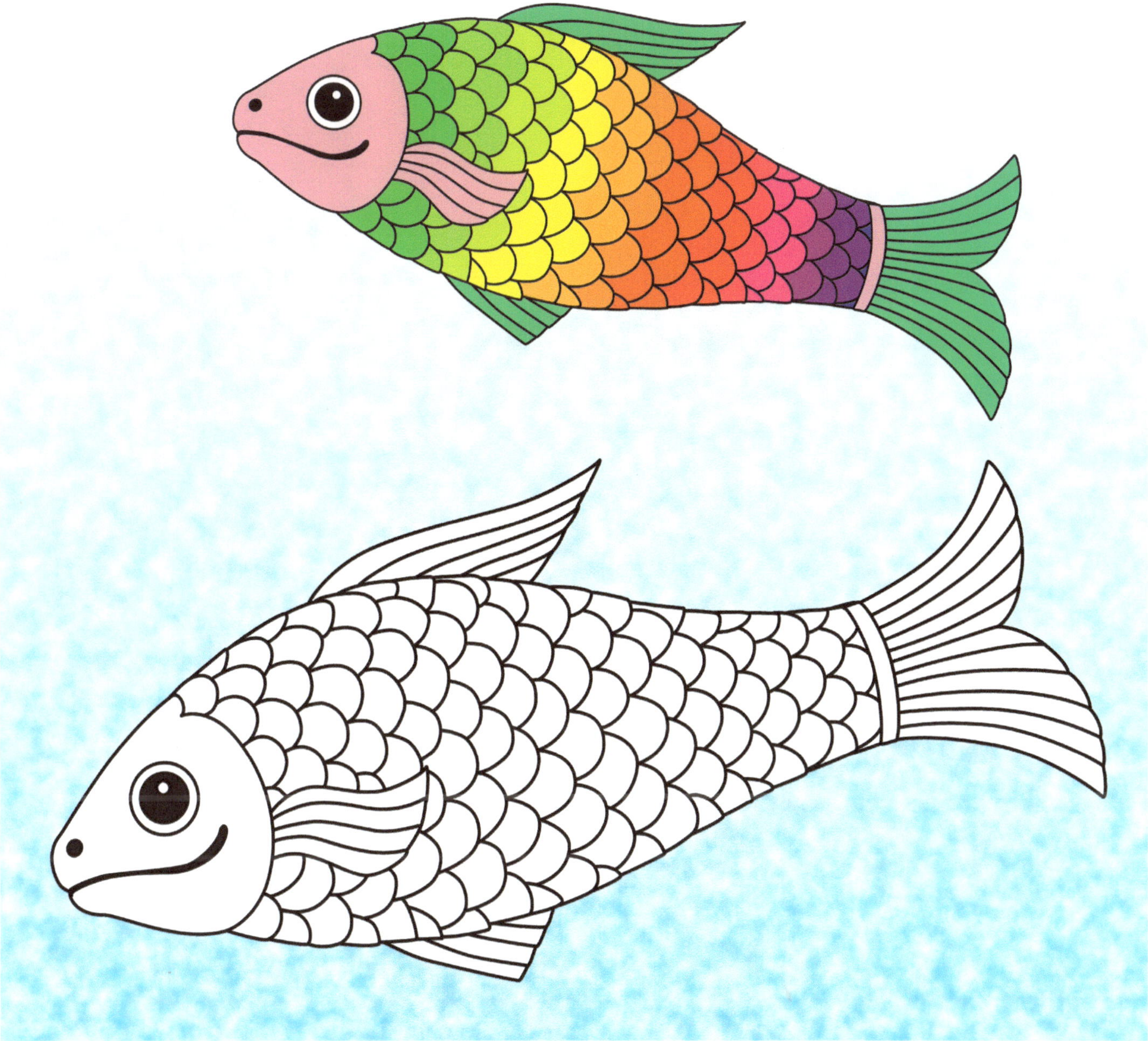

Swimming fish from a bas-relief in scenes on day-to-day life at the Bayon, Angkor Thom.

Color the drawings above using your preferred choice of colors.

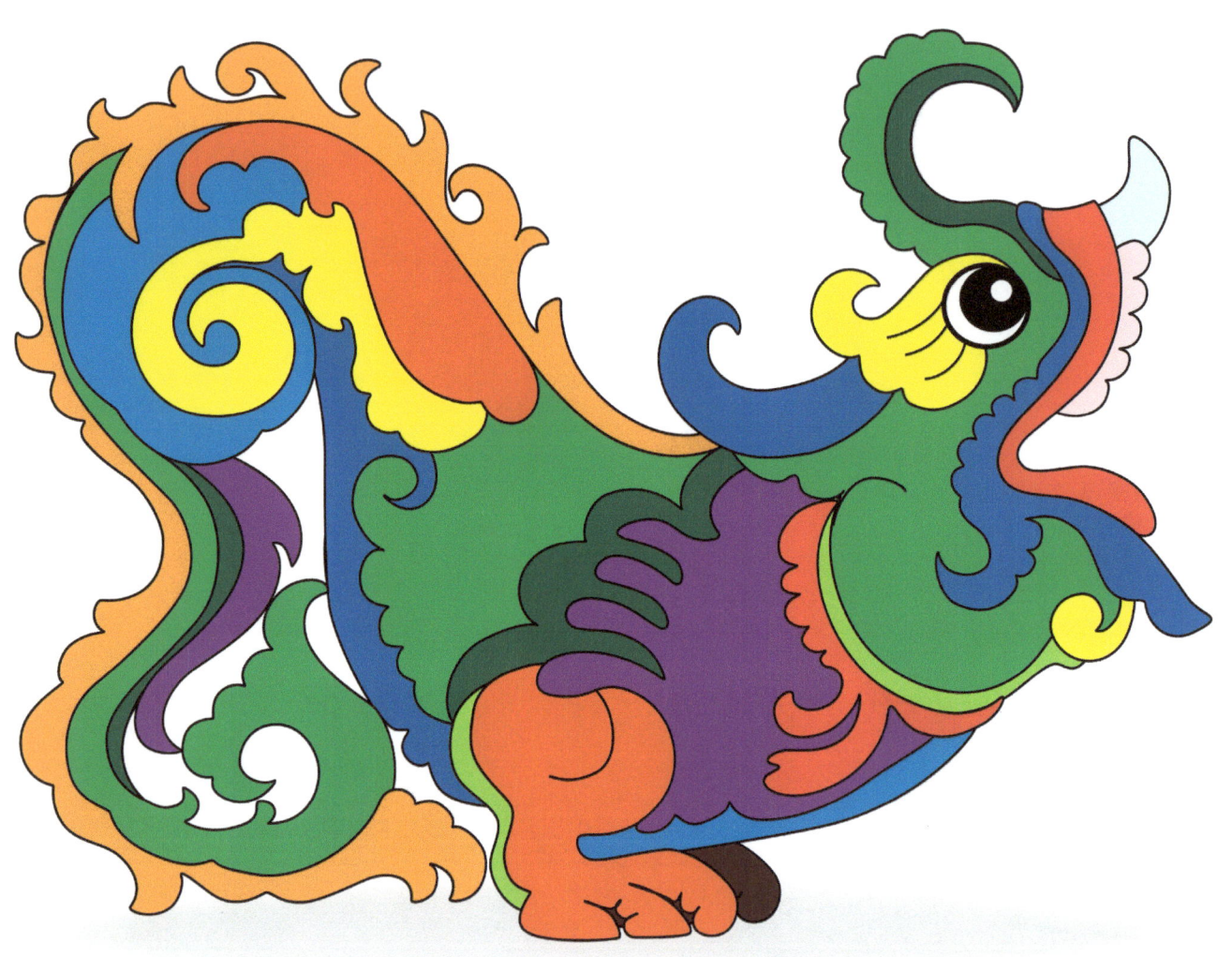

From drawings on lintel of the Sambor Prei style. Animal - probably a Makara.

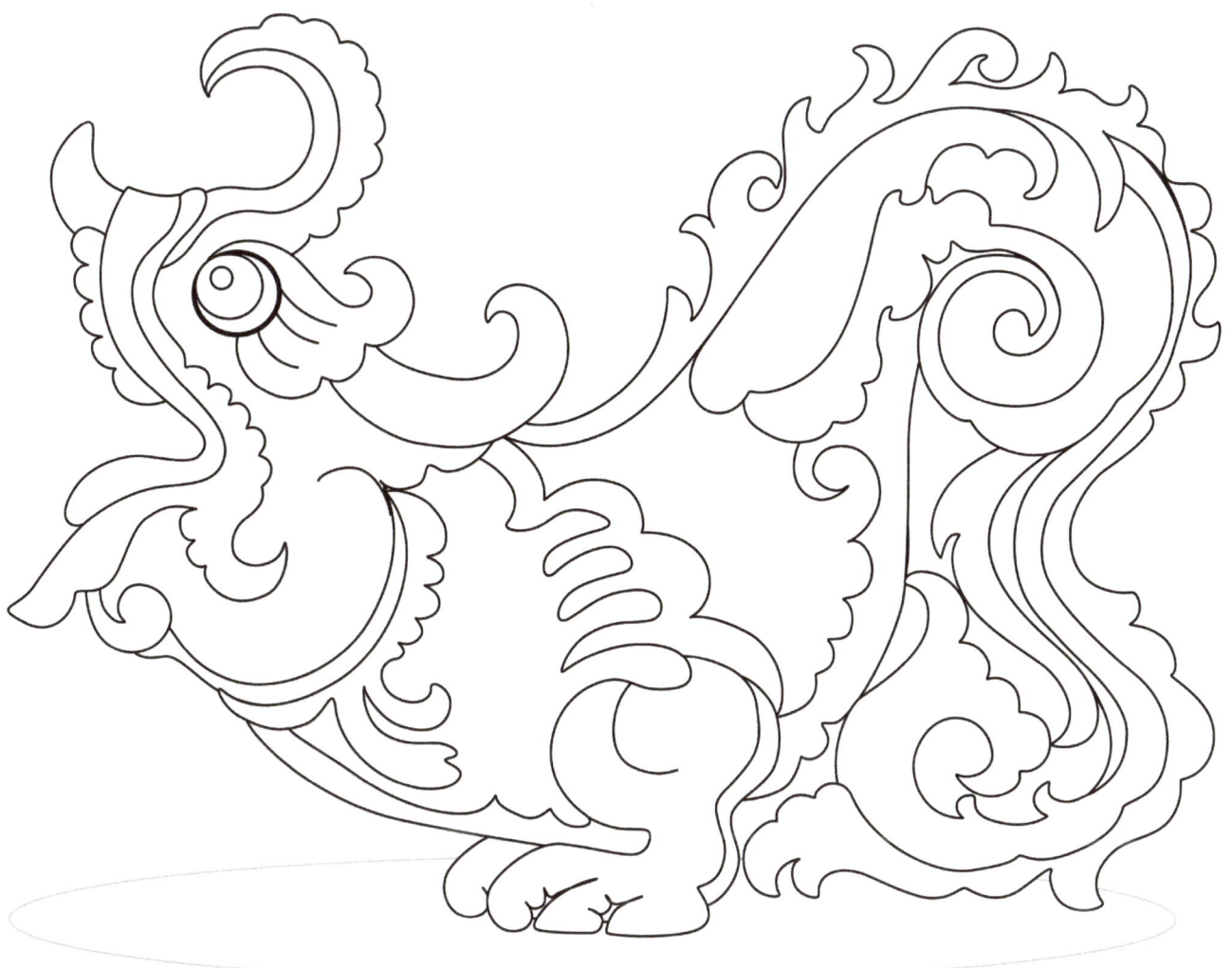

Color the drawing above using your preferred choice of colors.

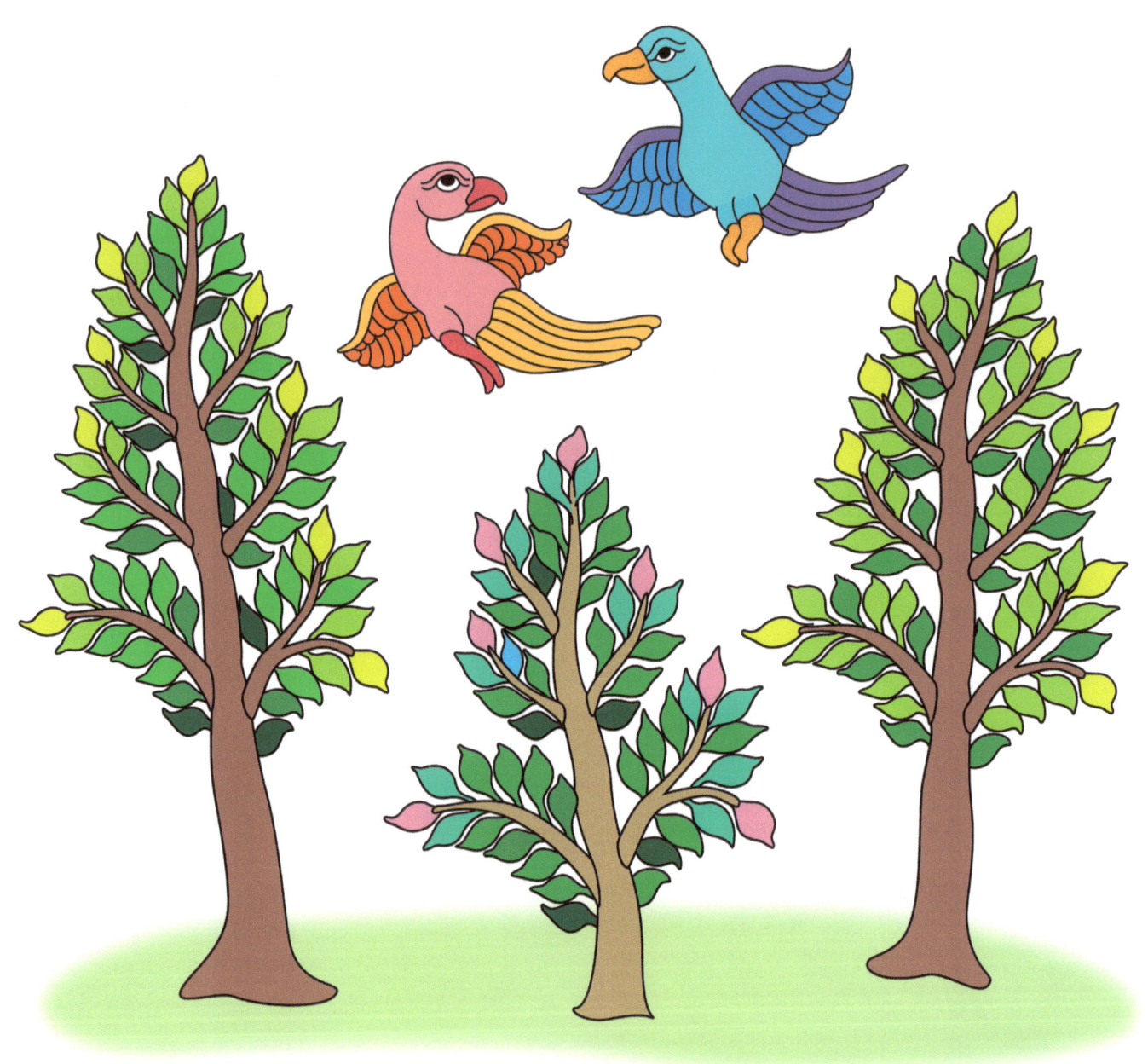

Birds and trees from reliefs of the eastern front
of the North "library." Banteay Srei, Angkor Wat, 967 C.E.

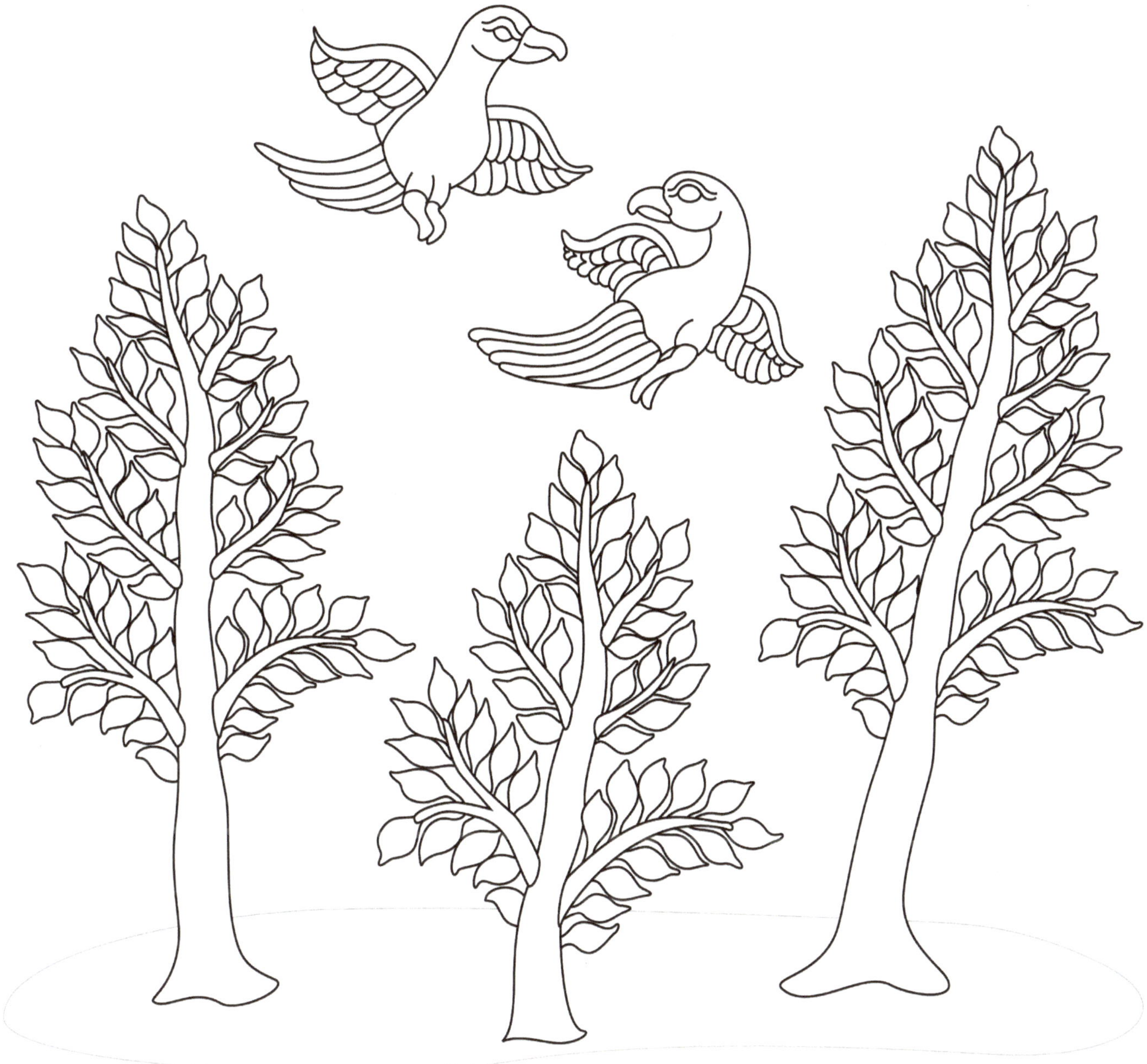

Color the drawings above using your preferred choice of colors.

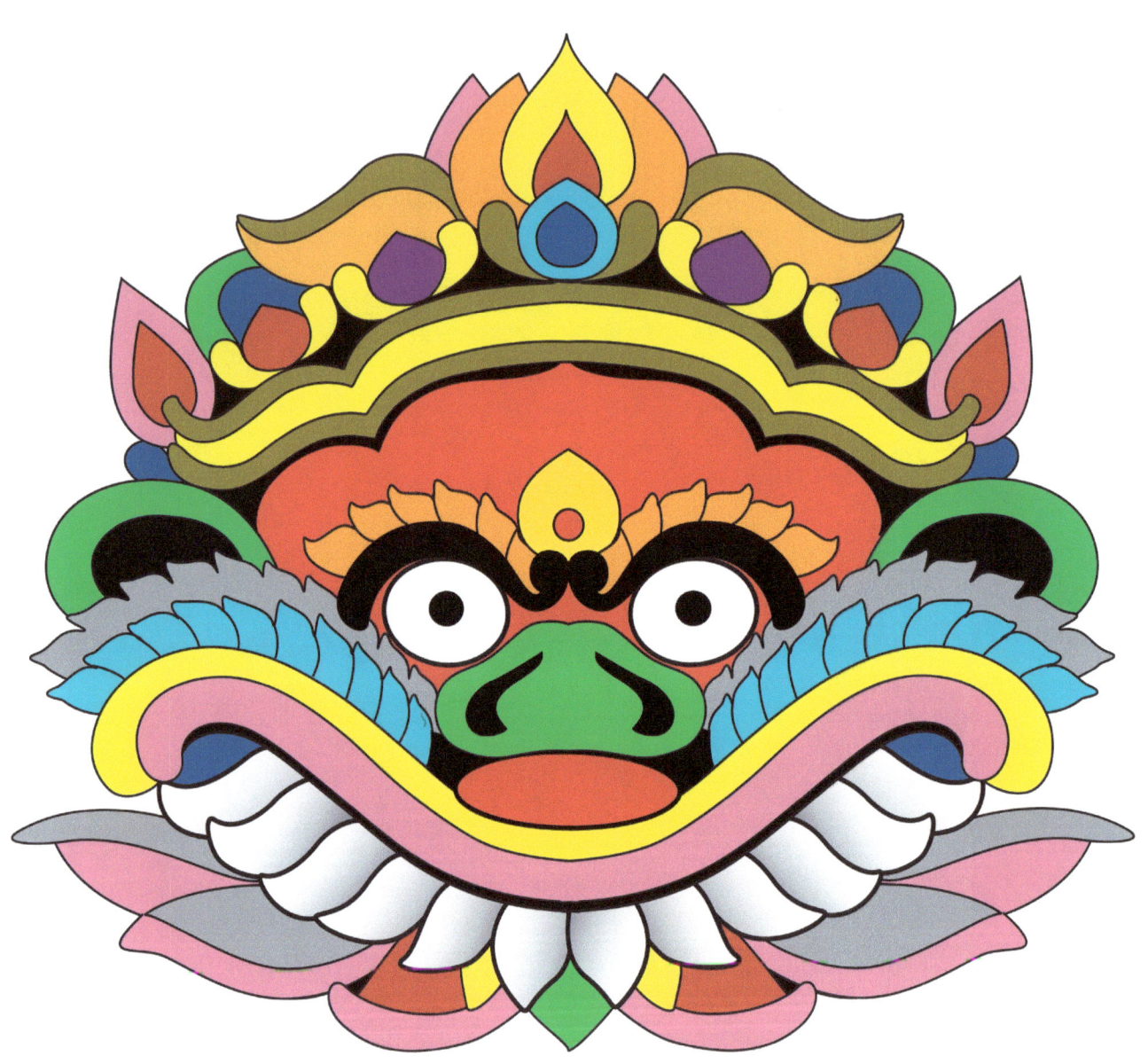

A Monster head on the gate of a temple in Banteay Srei. Angkor Wat, 11th Century C.E.

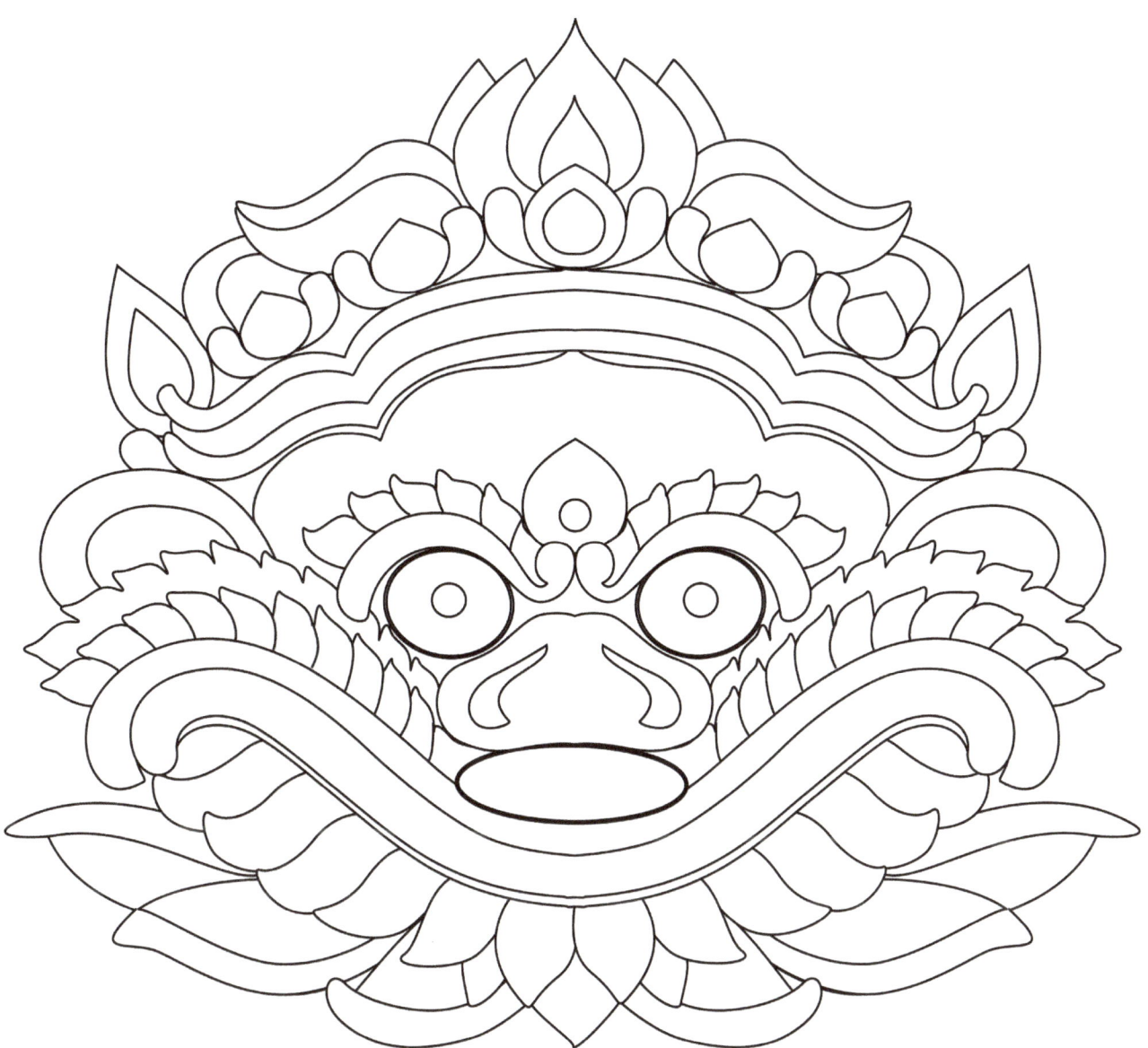

Color the drawing above using your preferred choice of colors.

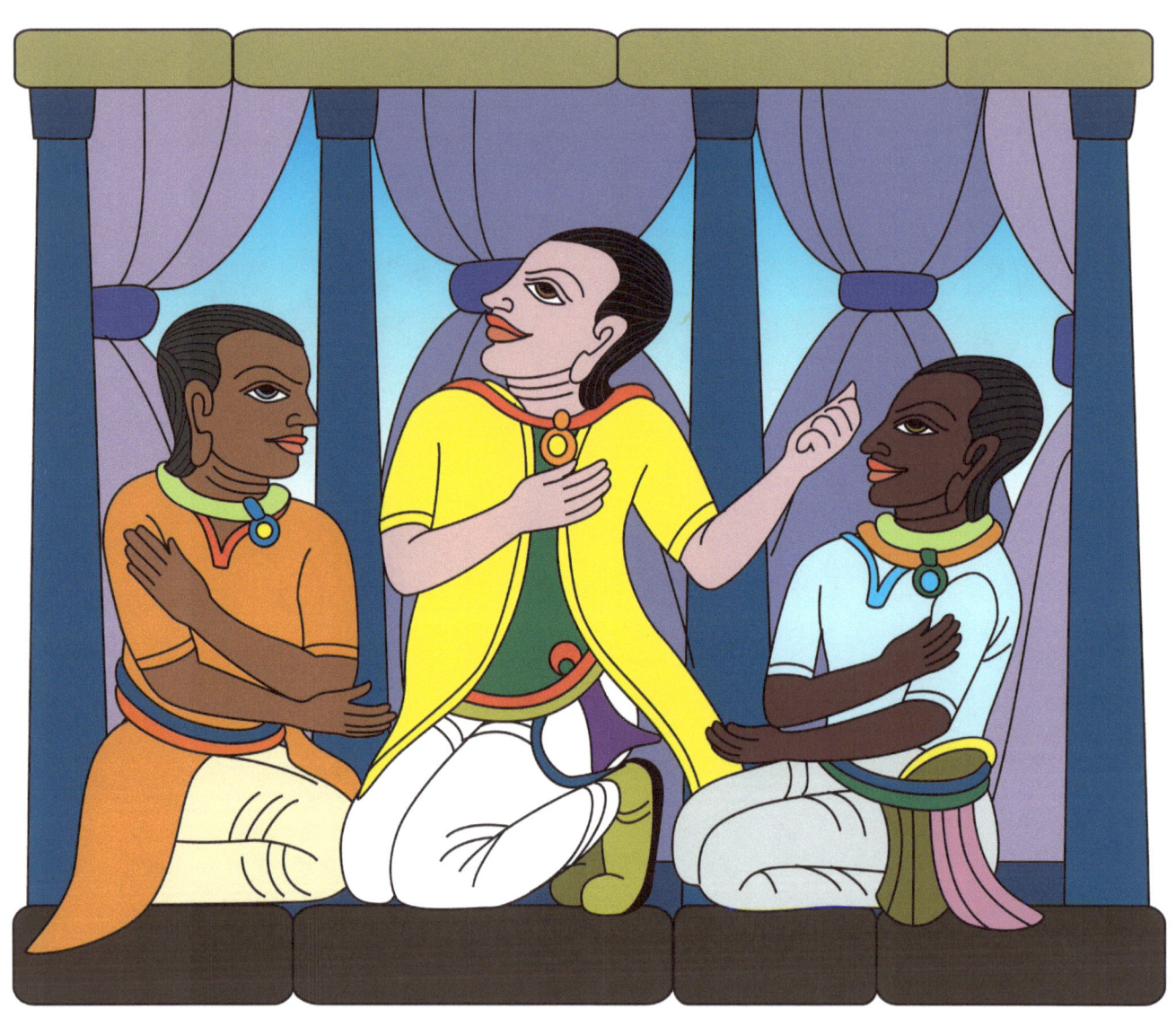

Bas-relief on the outer gallery, The Bayon. Representing the celebration of victory.

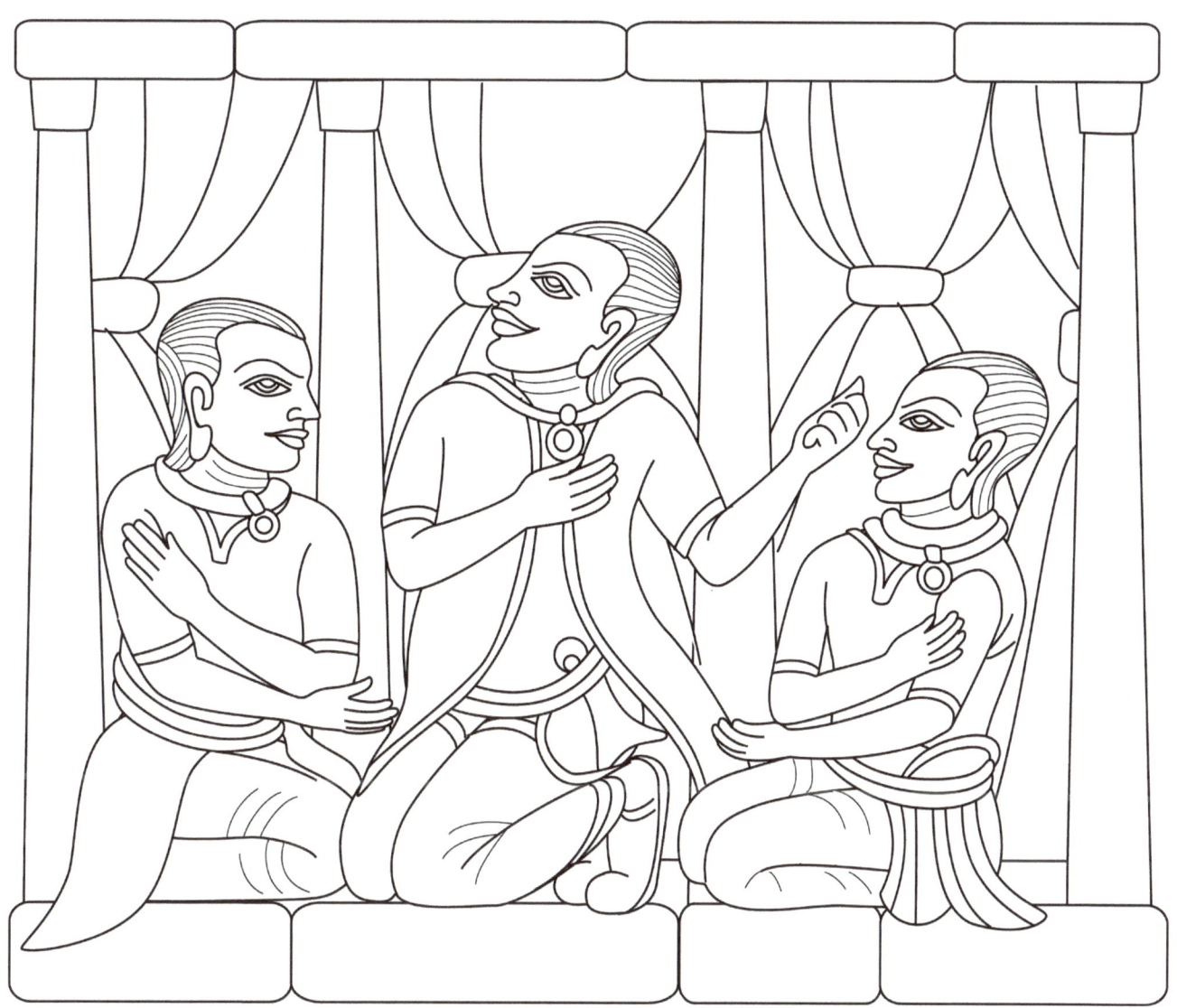

Color the drawing above using your preferred choice of colors.

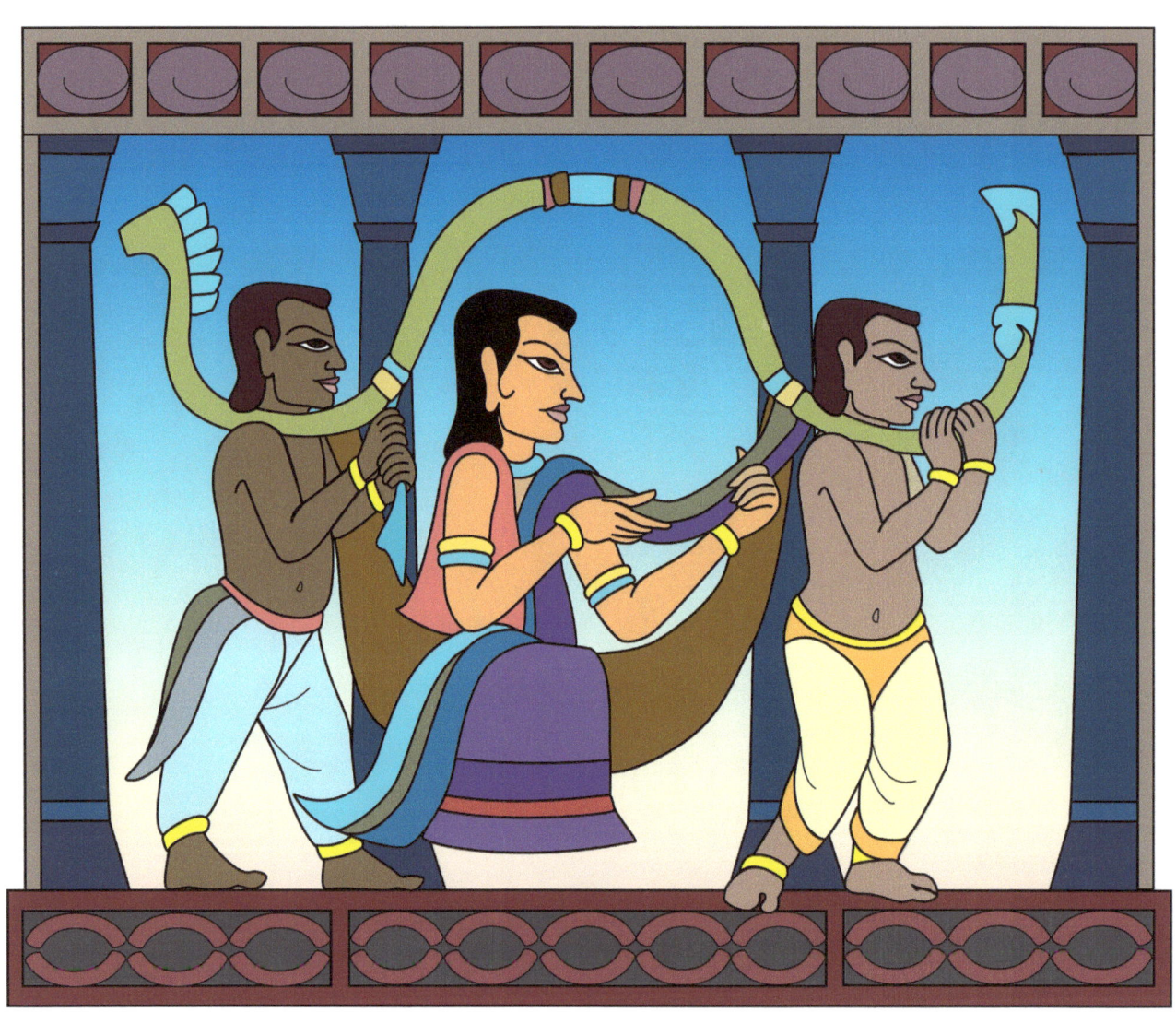

A relief showing one person is carried on a palanquin. The same type of palanquin was in use throughout Indo-Chinese up to the beginning of 20th Century C.E. The Bayon, Angkor Thom.

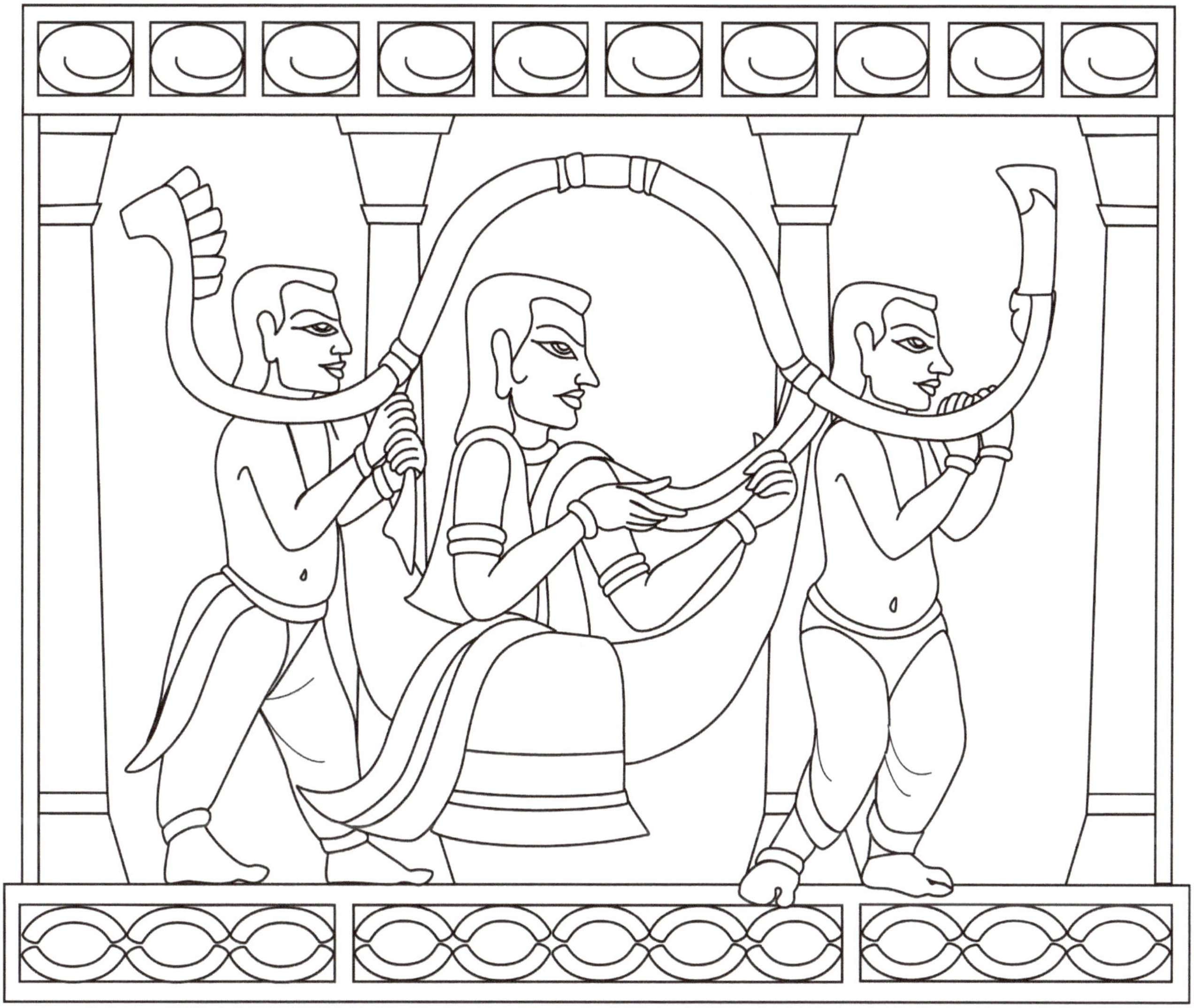

Color the drawing above using your preferred choice of colors.

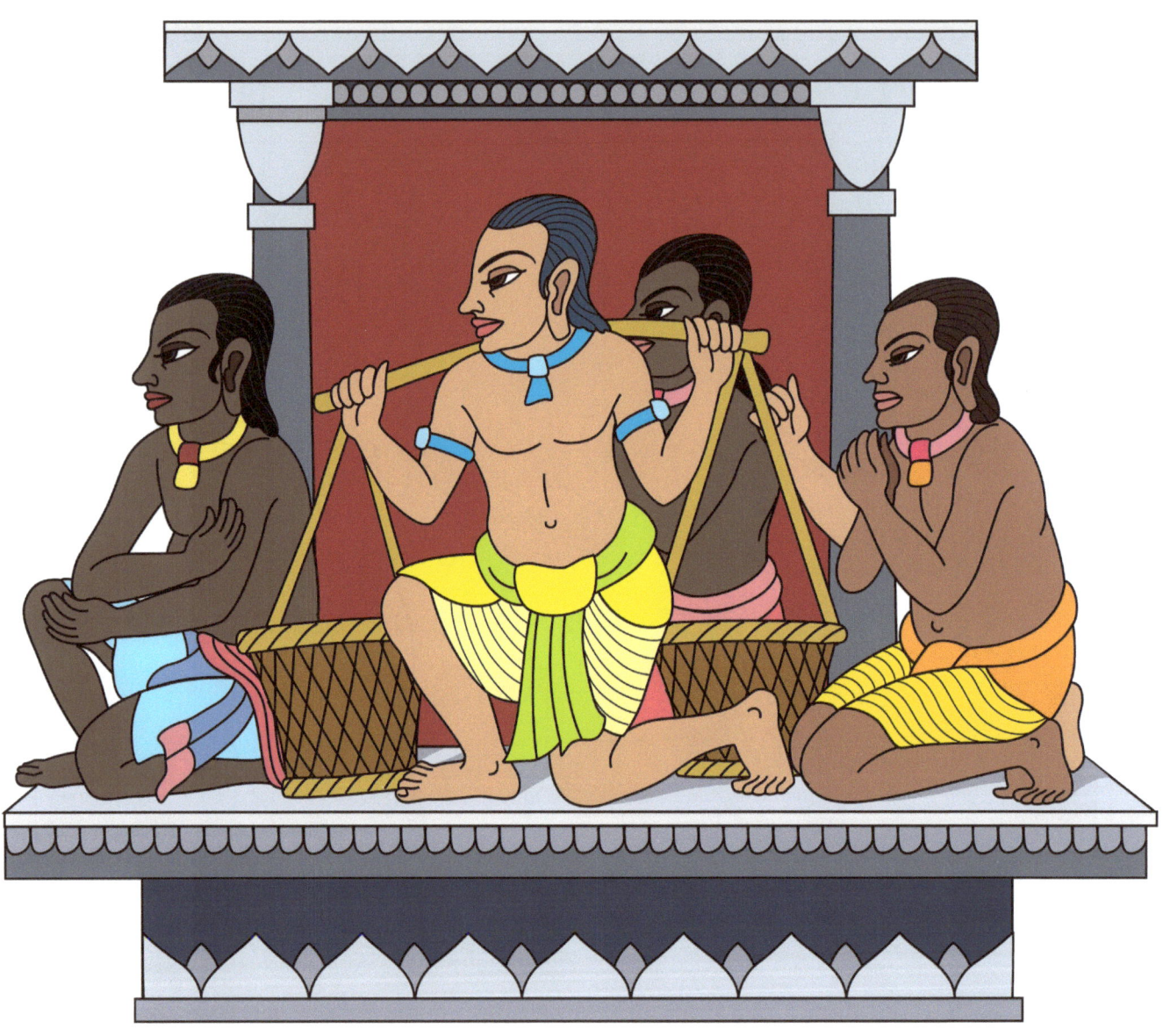

An episode from the daily life on a bas-relief in the temple of the Bayon.

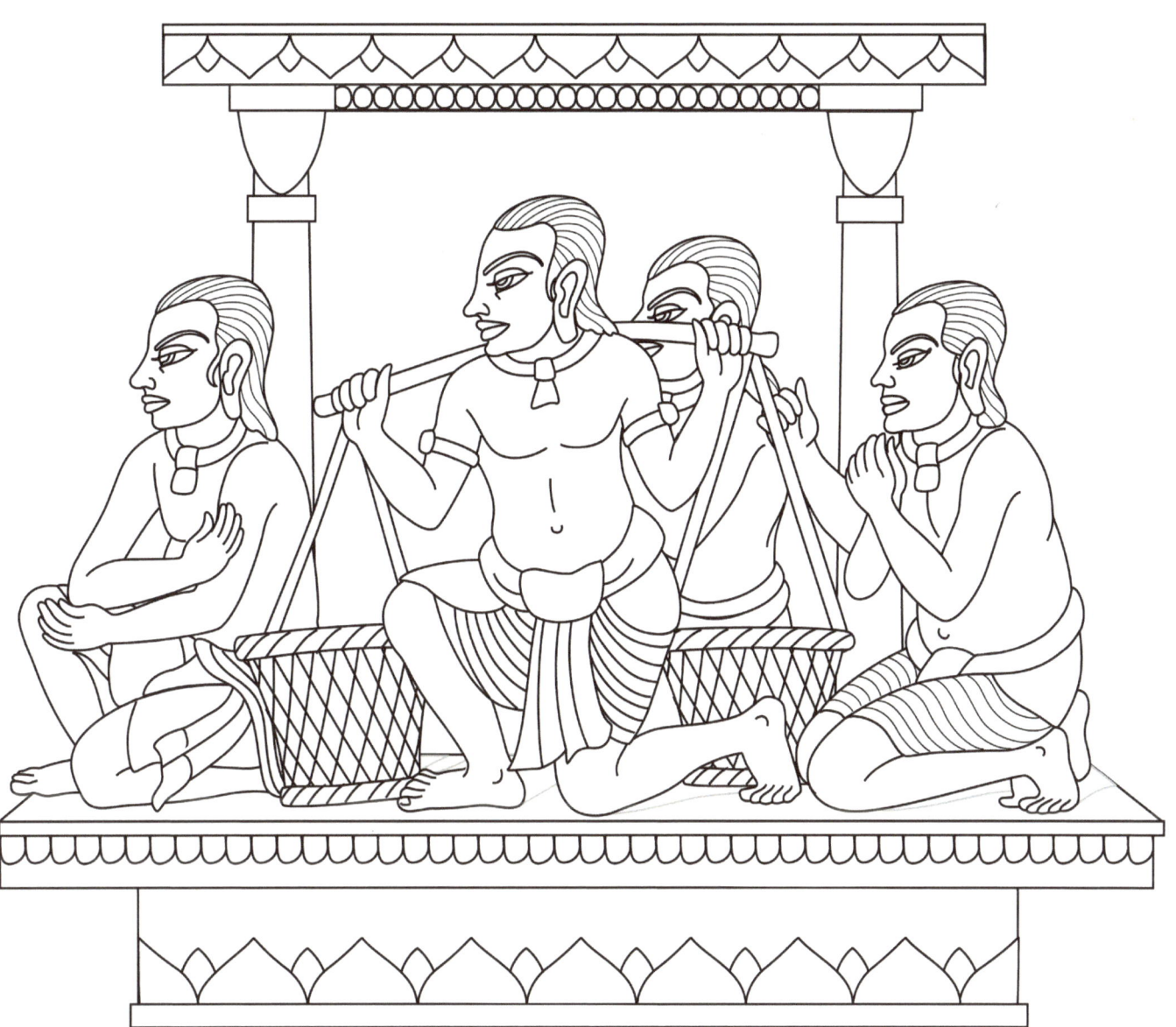

Color the drawing above using your preferred choice of colors.

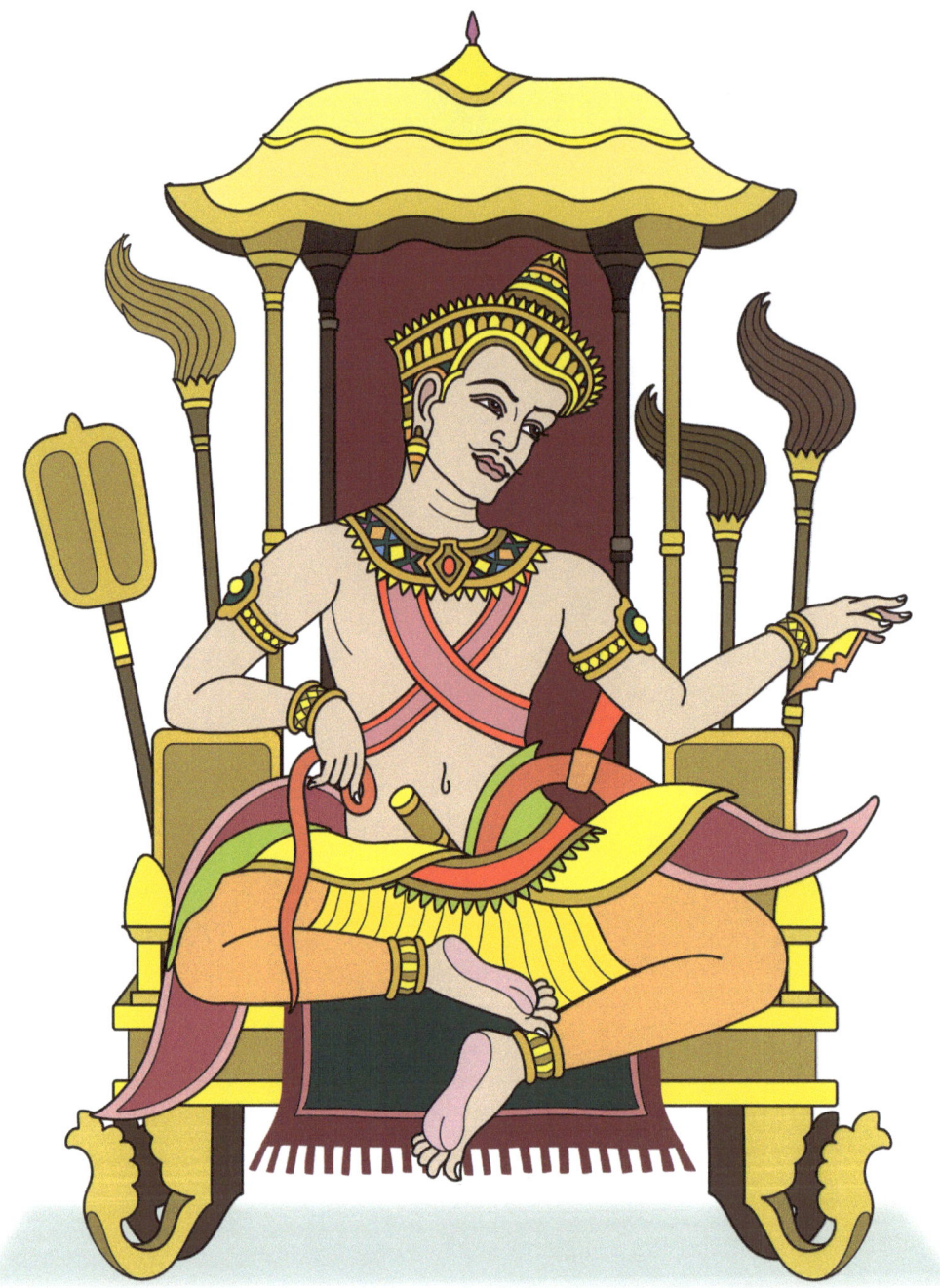

King Suryavarman -II in his throne. Angkor Vat.

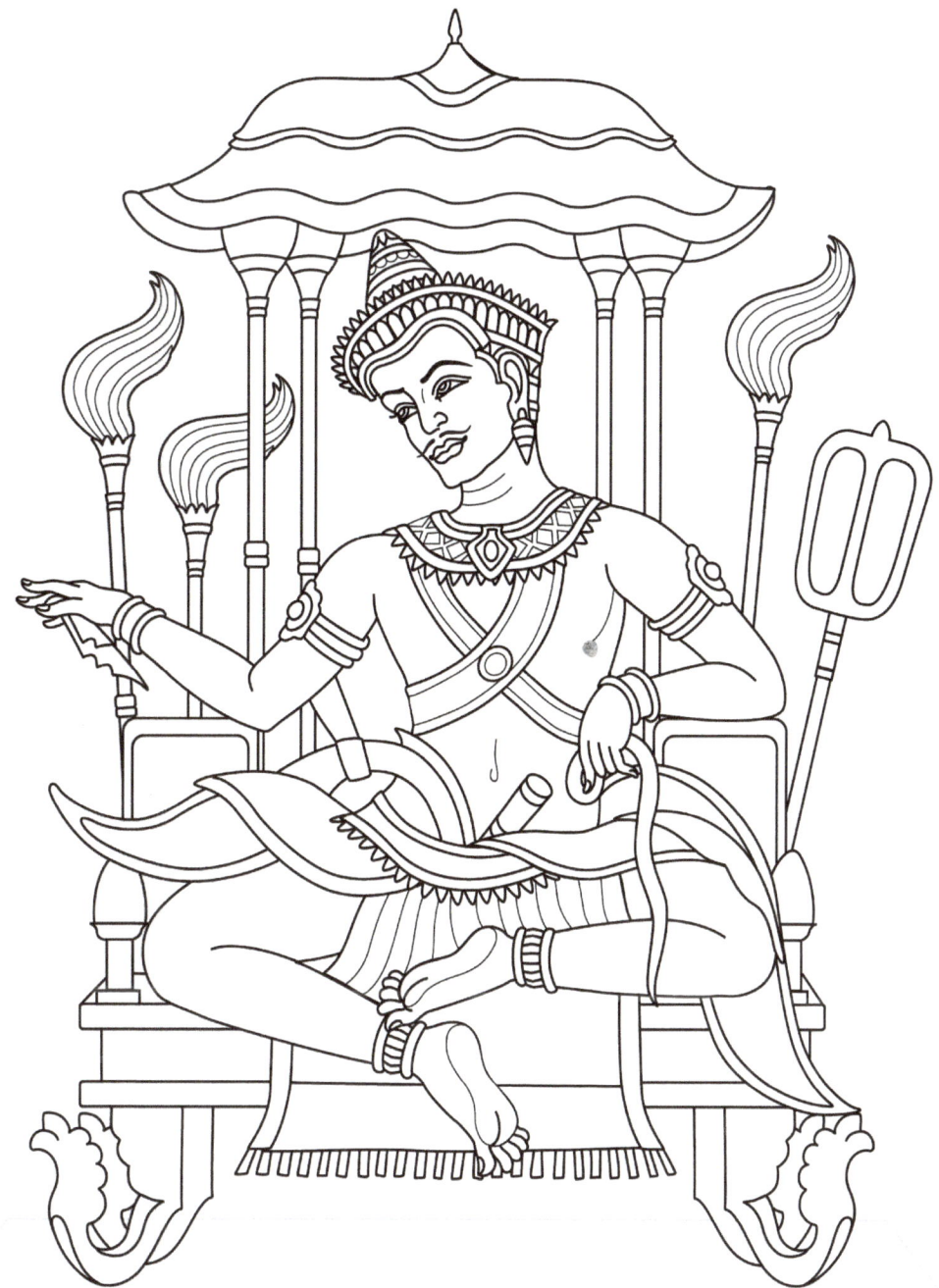

Color the drawing above using your preferred choice of colors.

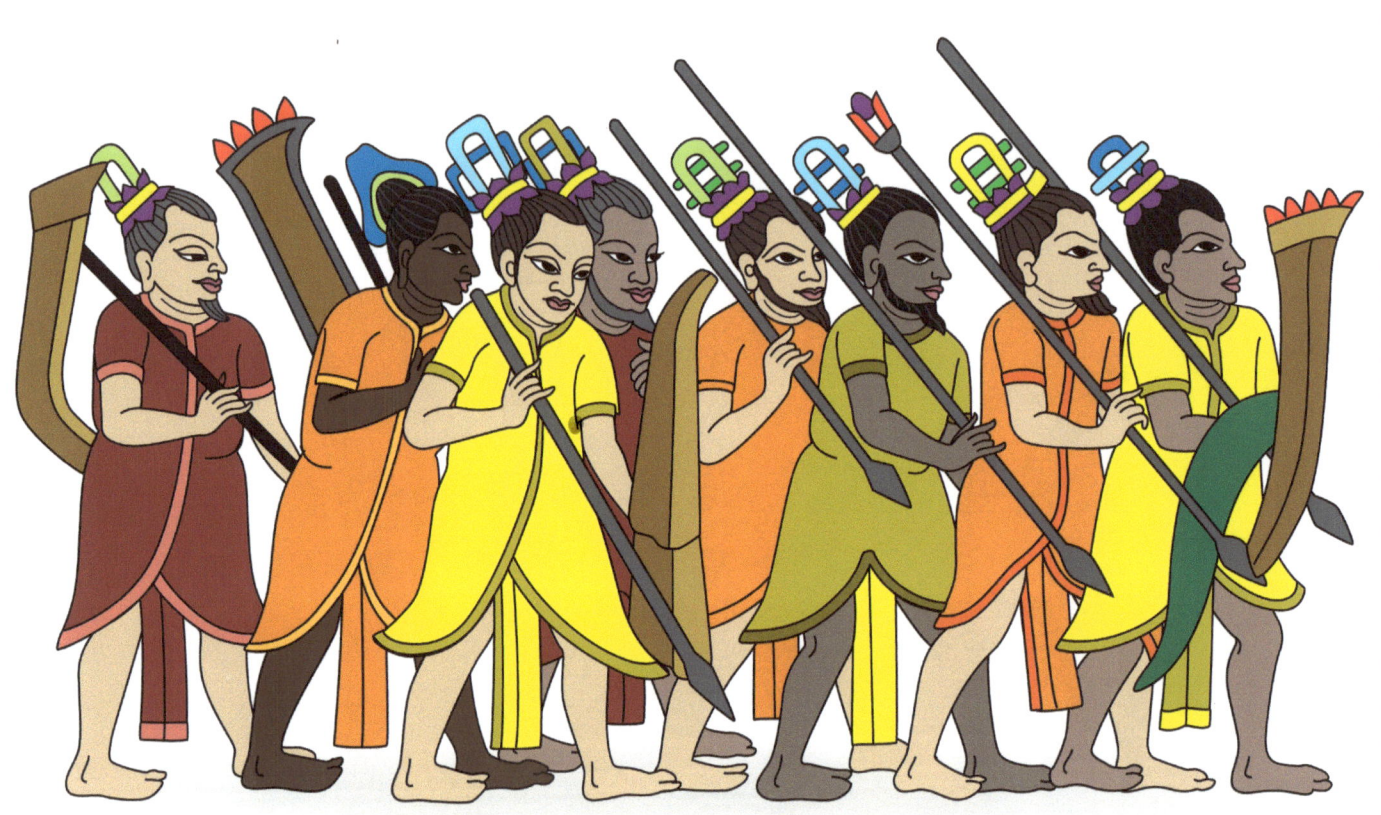

The army of Chams, from the relief in the outer gallery.
The Bayon, Angkor Thom. Towards the end of 12th Century C.E.

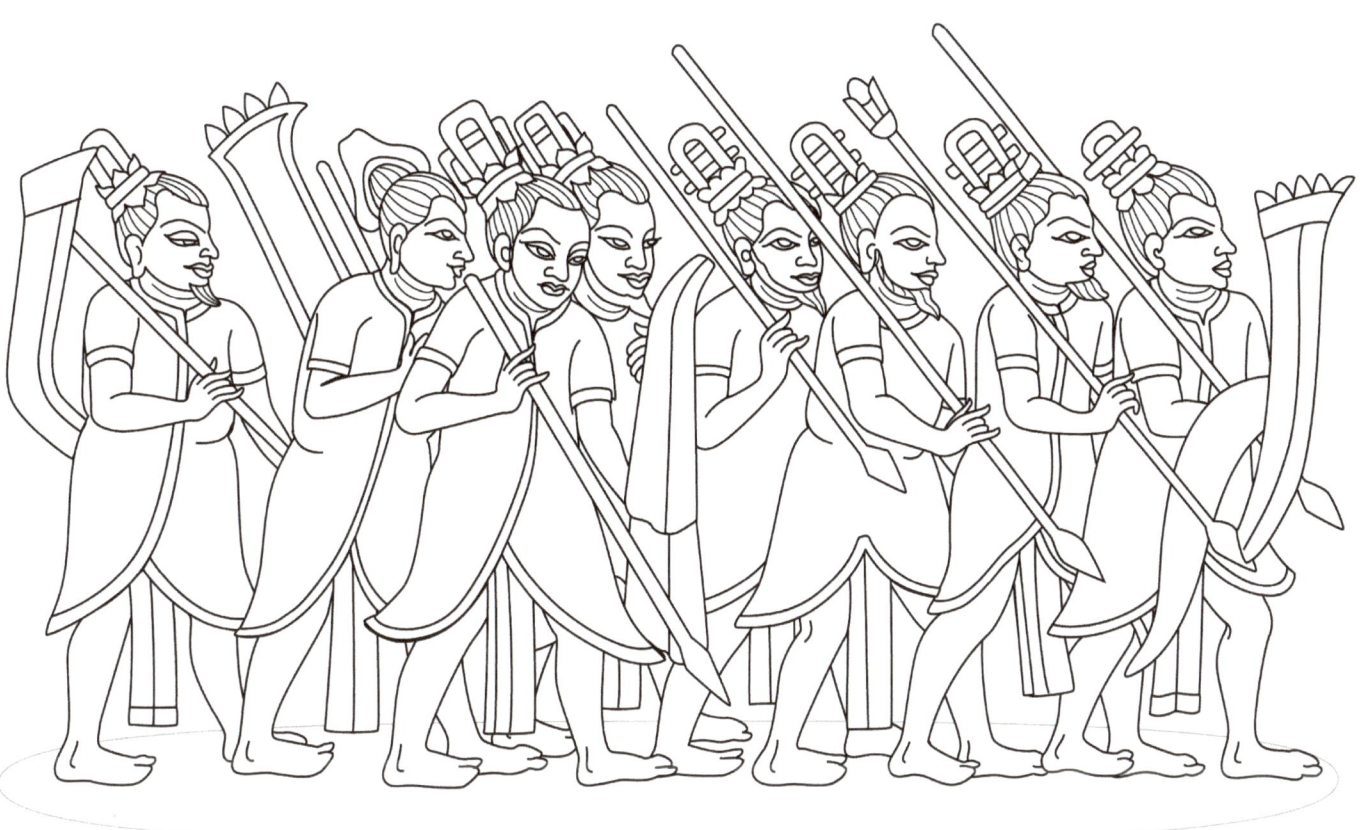

Color the drawing above using your preferred choice of colors.

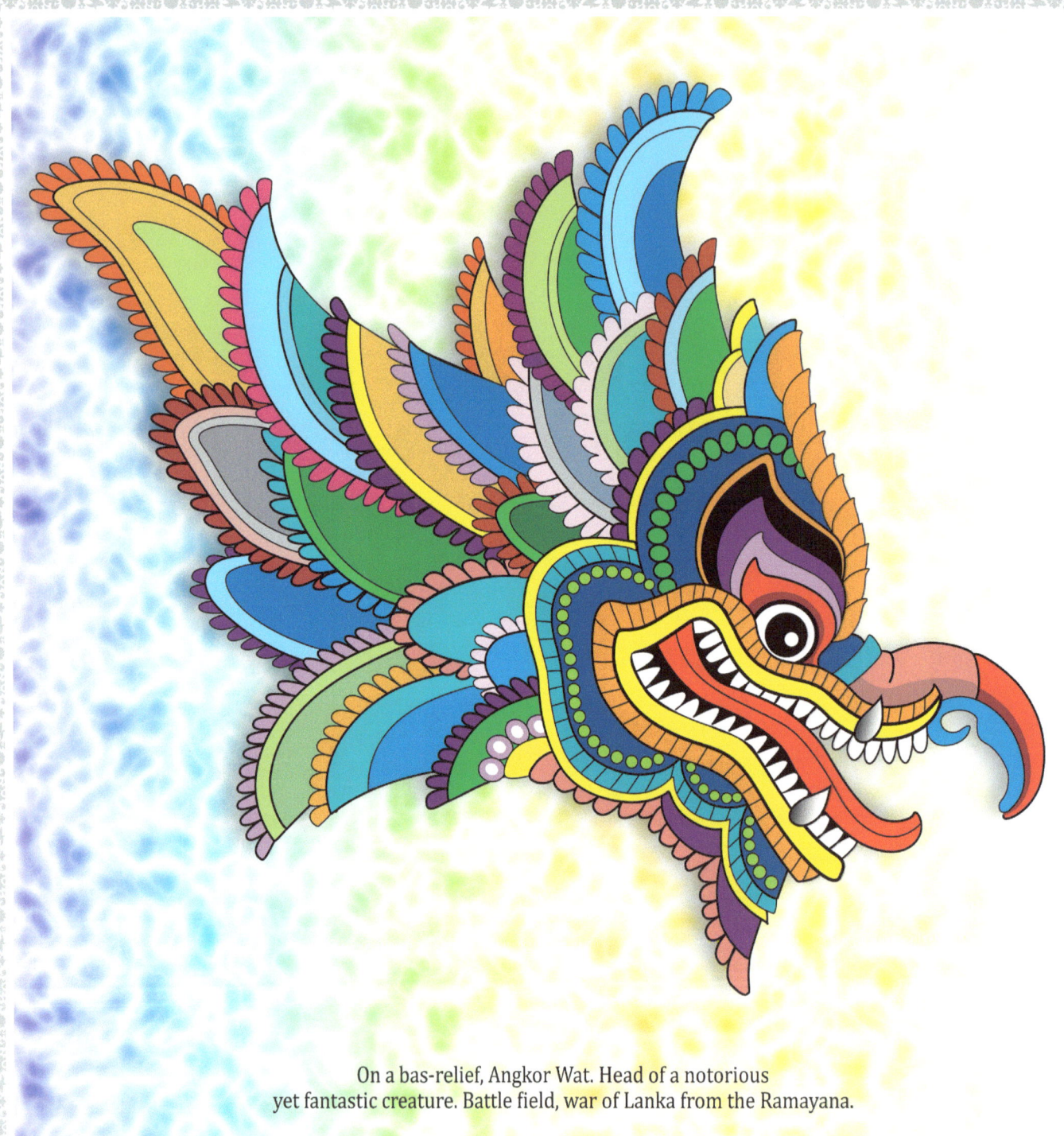

On a bas-relief, Angkor Wat. Head of a notorious
yet fantastic creature. Battle field, war of Lanka from the Ramayana.

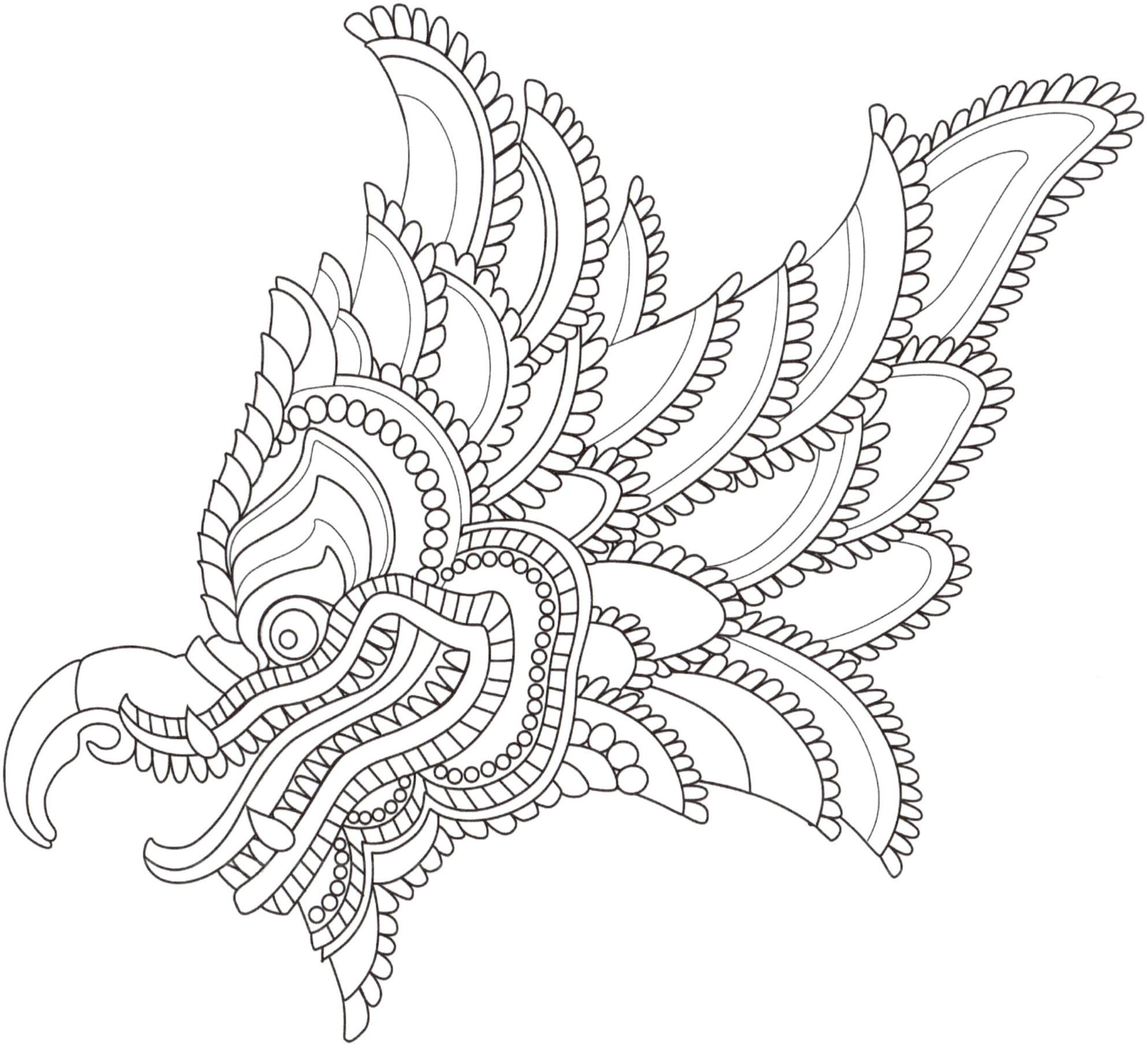

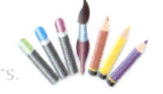

Color the drawing above using your preferred choice of colors.

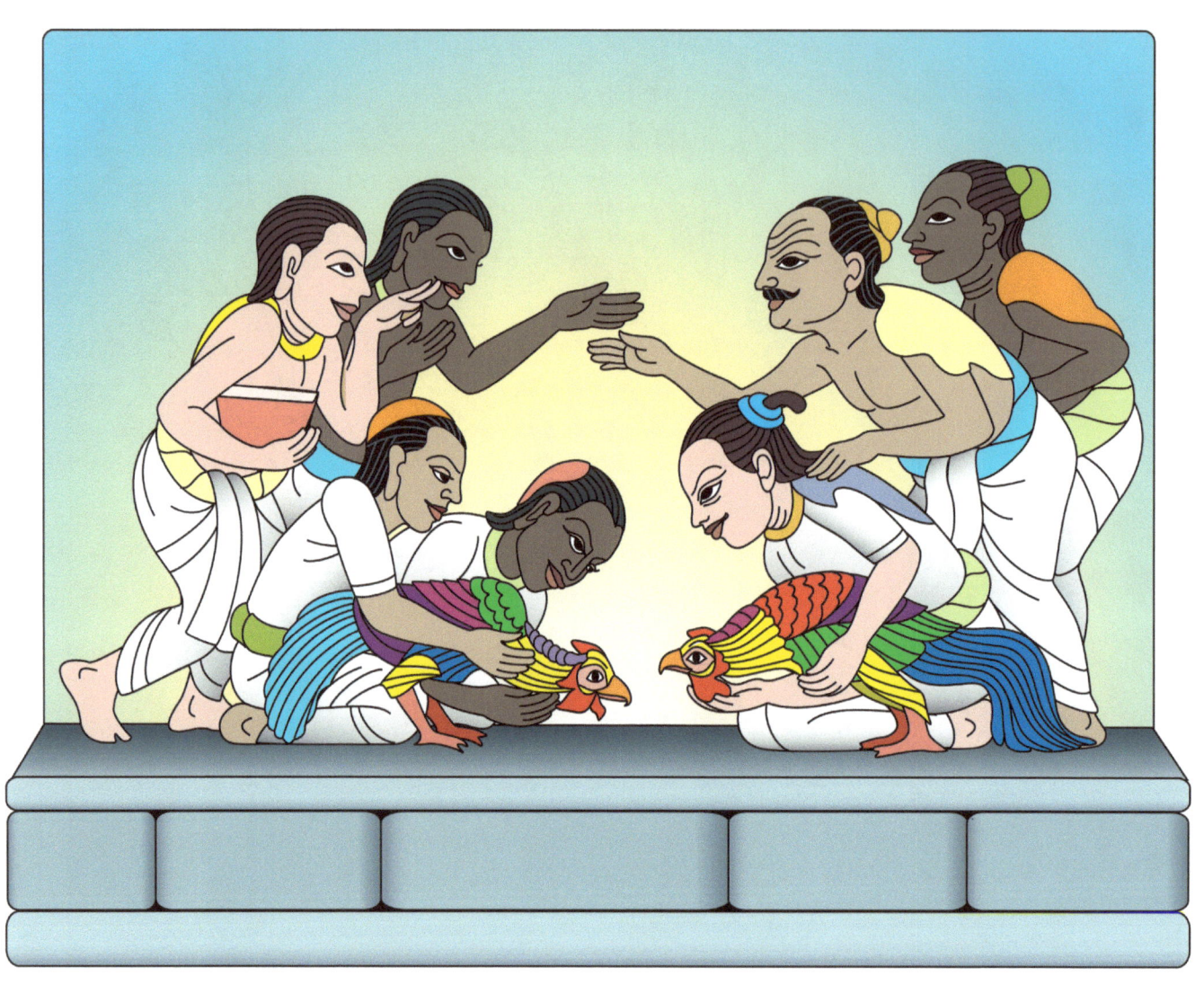

Bas-relief of a cockfight in the outer gallery of a temple at Angkor Thom.
First half of the 13th Century C.E. The scene is marked by remarkable vivacity
and the artist's ability to fit various figures into a limited space.

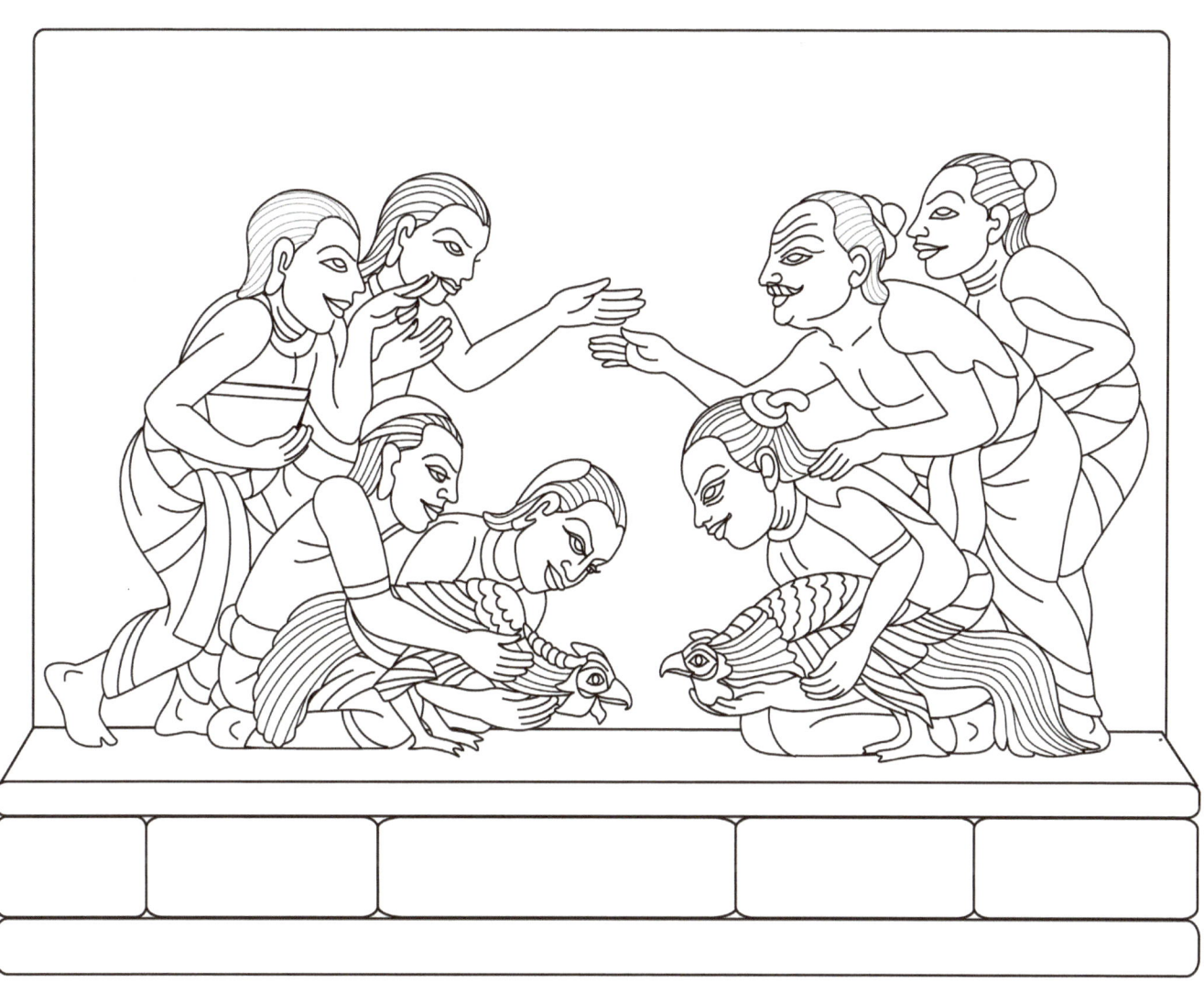

Color the drawing above using your preferred choice of colors.

29

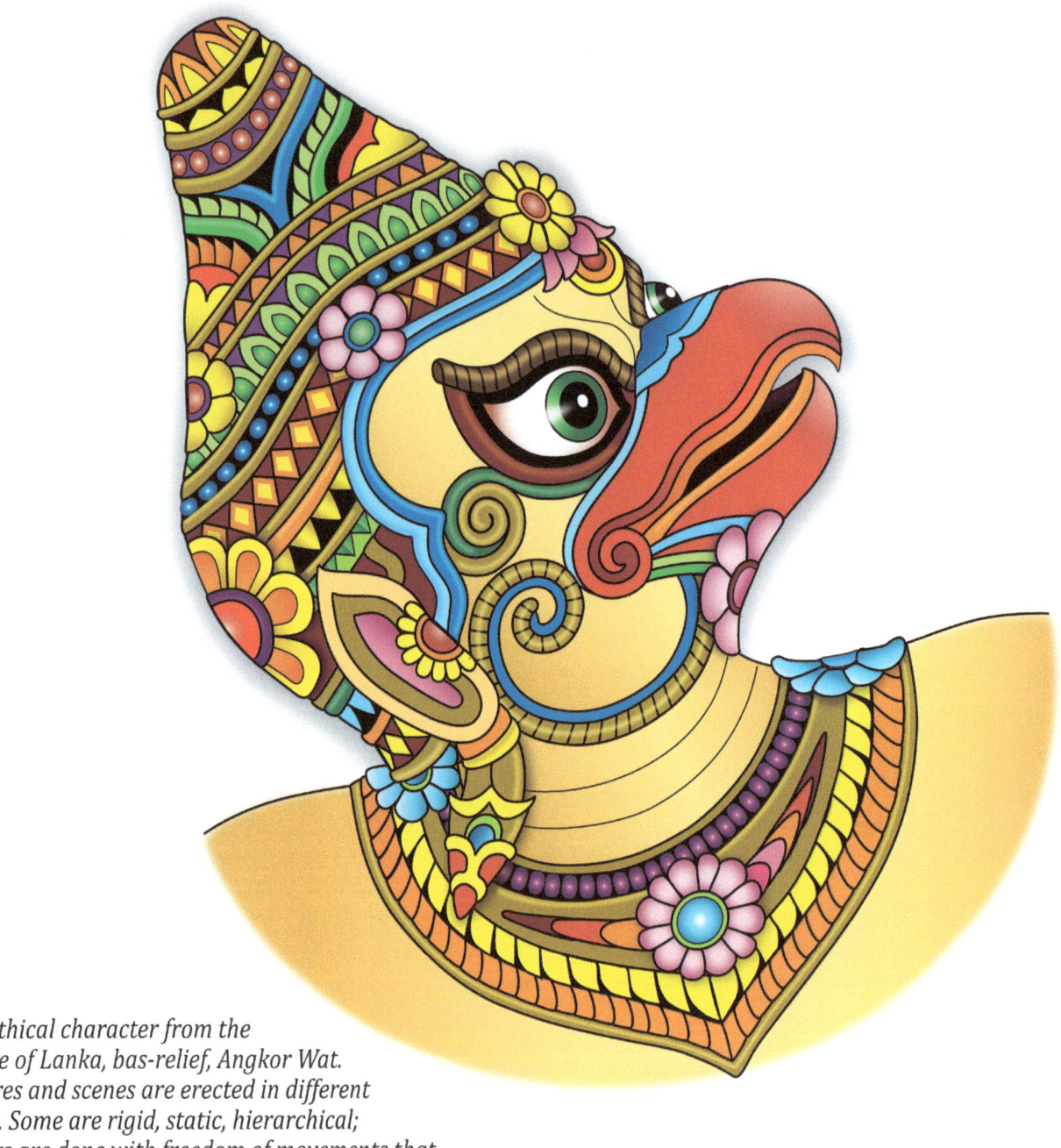

A Mythical character from the Battle of Lanka, bas-relief, Angkor Wat. Figures and scenes are erected in different ways. Some are rigid, static, hierarchical; others are done with freedom of movements that transmit a dynamism to everything around them.

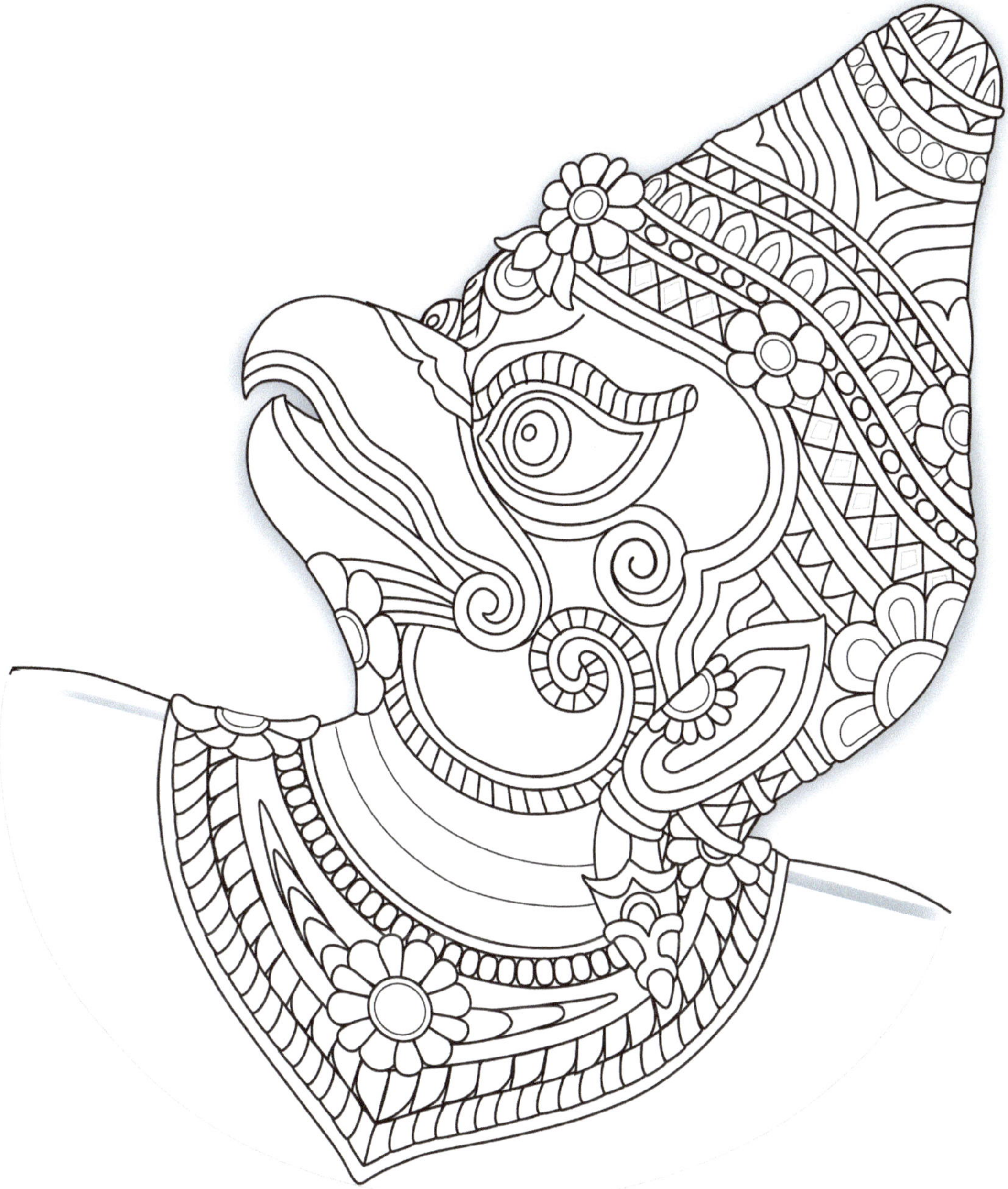

Color the drawing above using your preferred choice of colors.

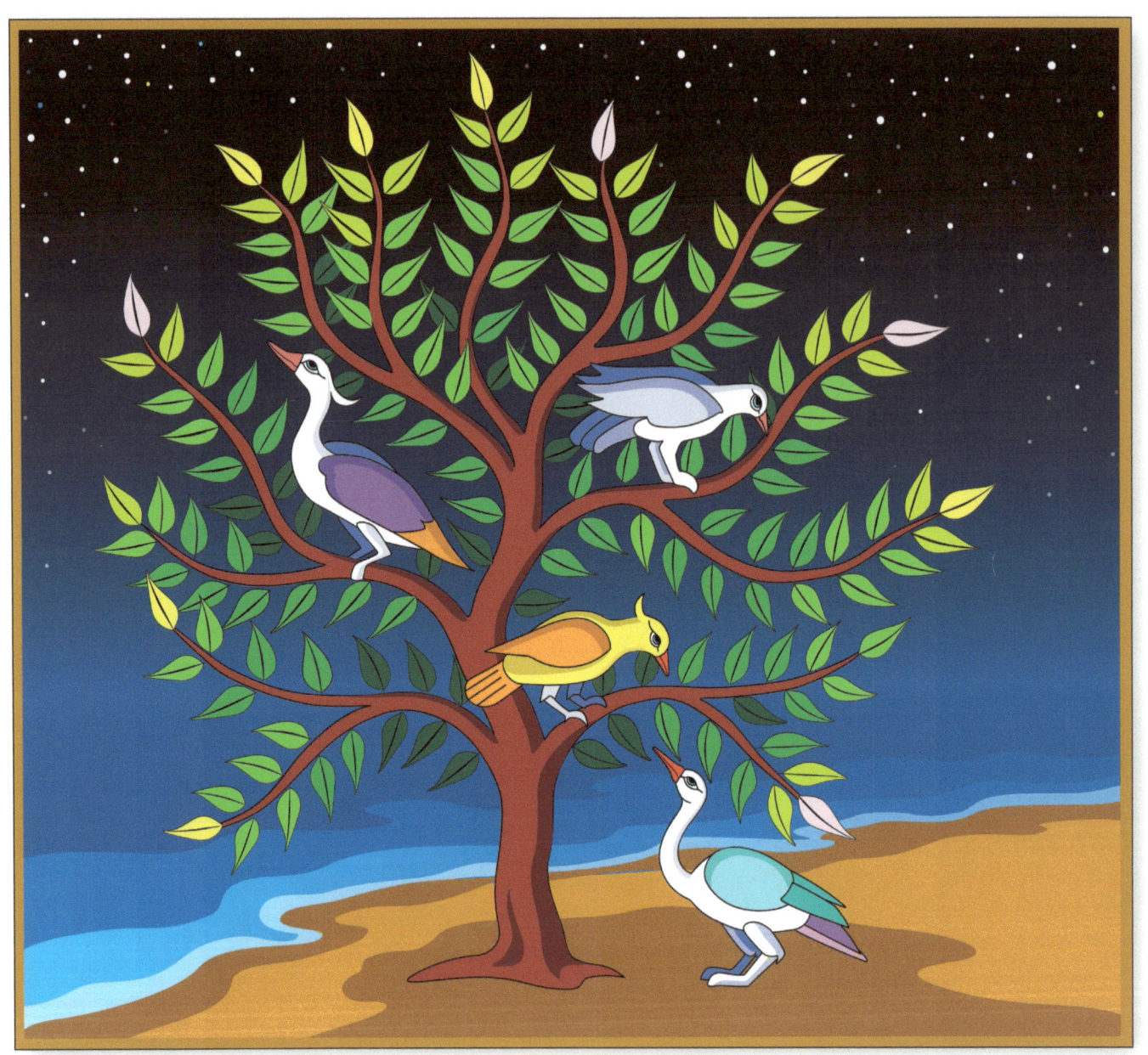

Beautiful birds, from bas-relief on the North "library" at Banteay Srei, Angkor Wat.

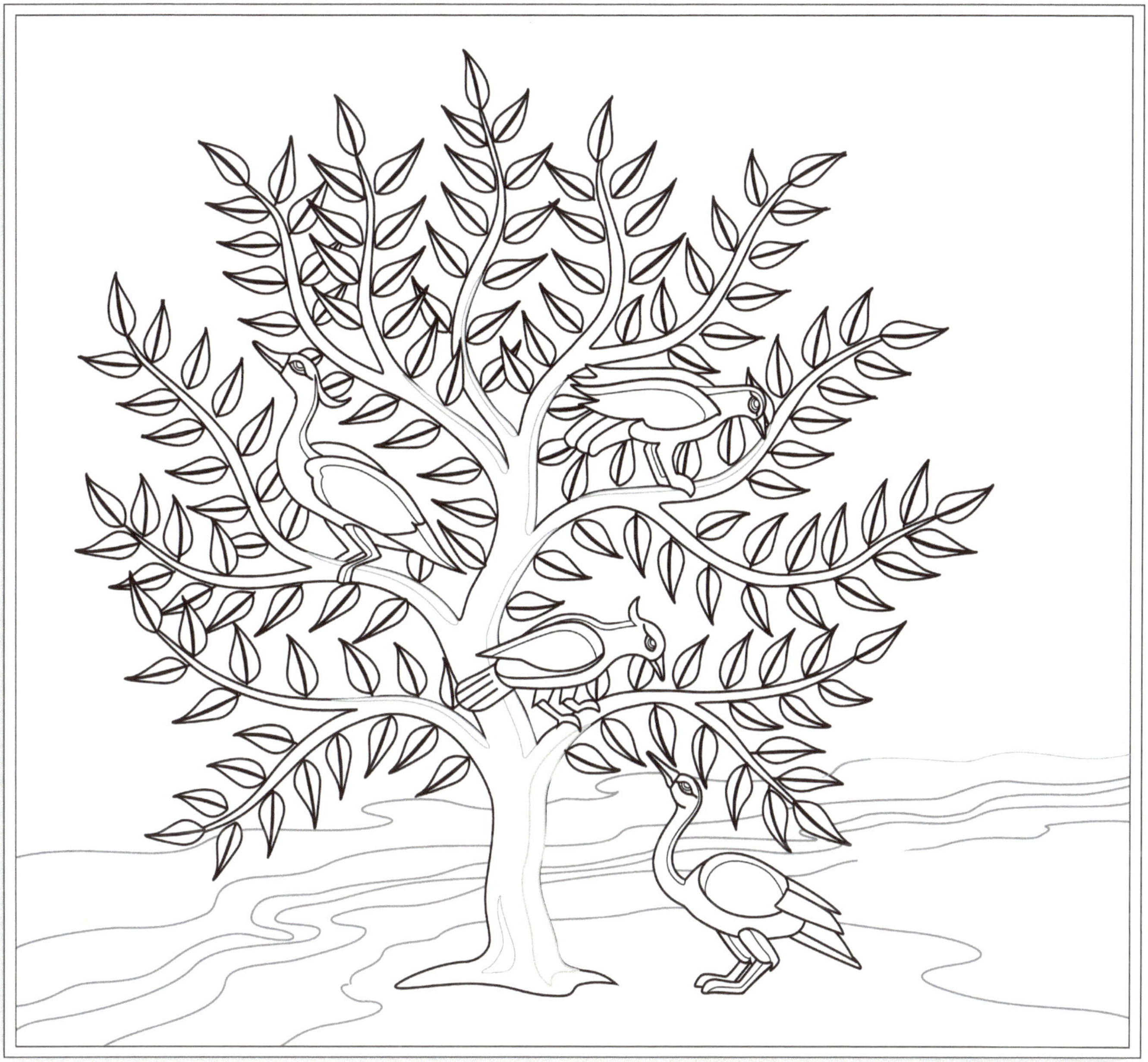

Color the drawing above using your preferred choice of colors.

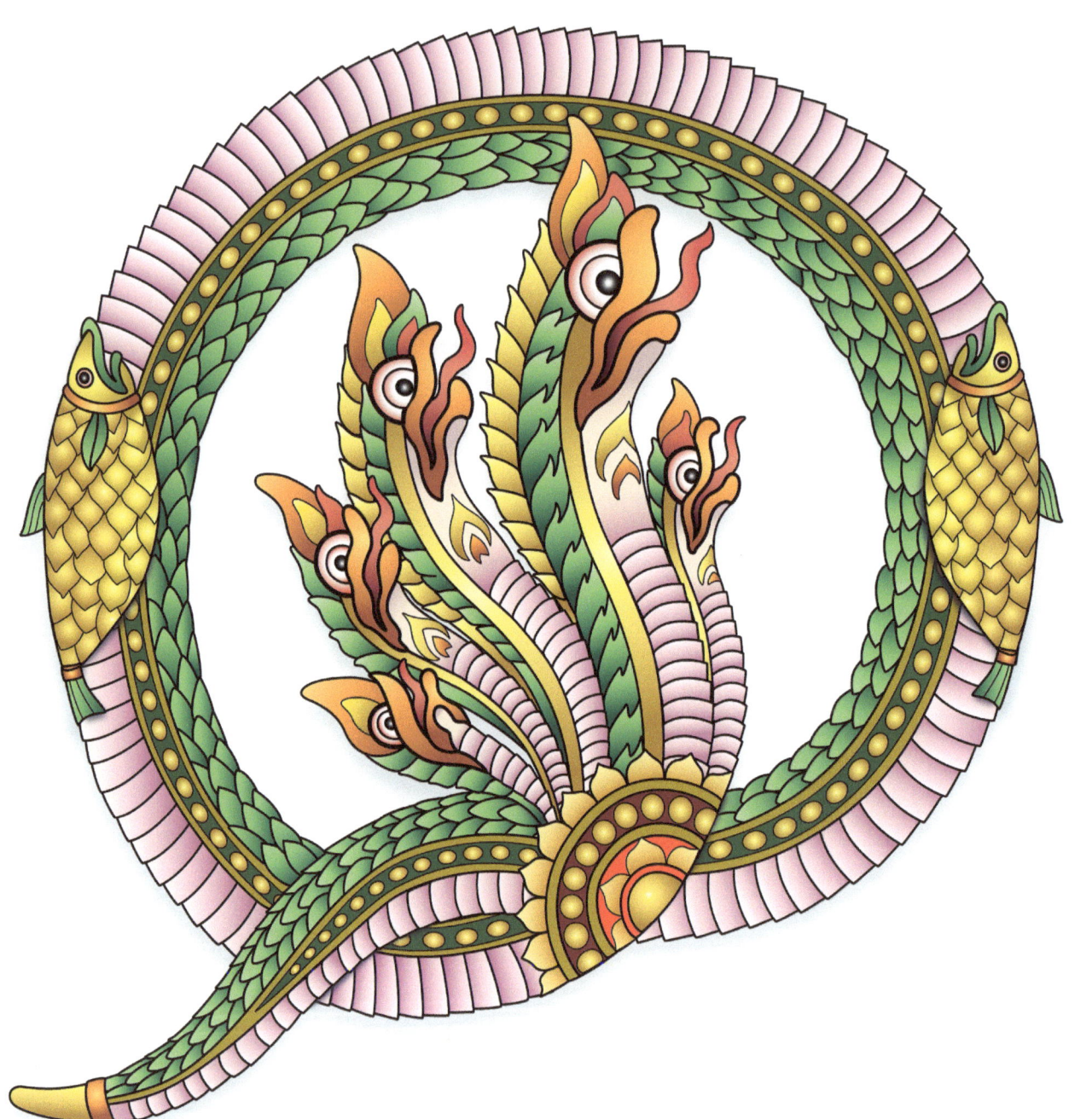

Bas-relief of the Snake God with five heads. Angkor Vat.

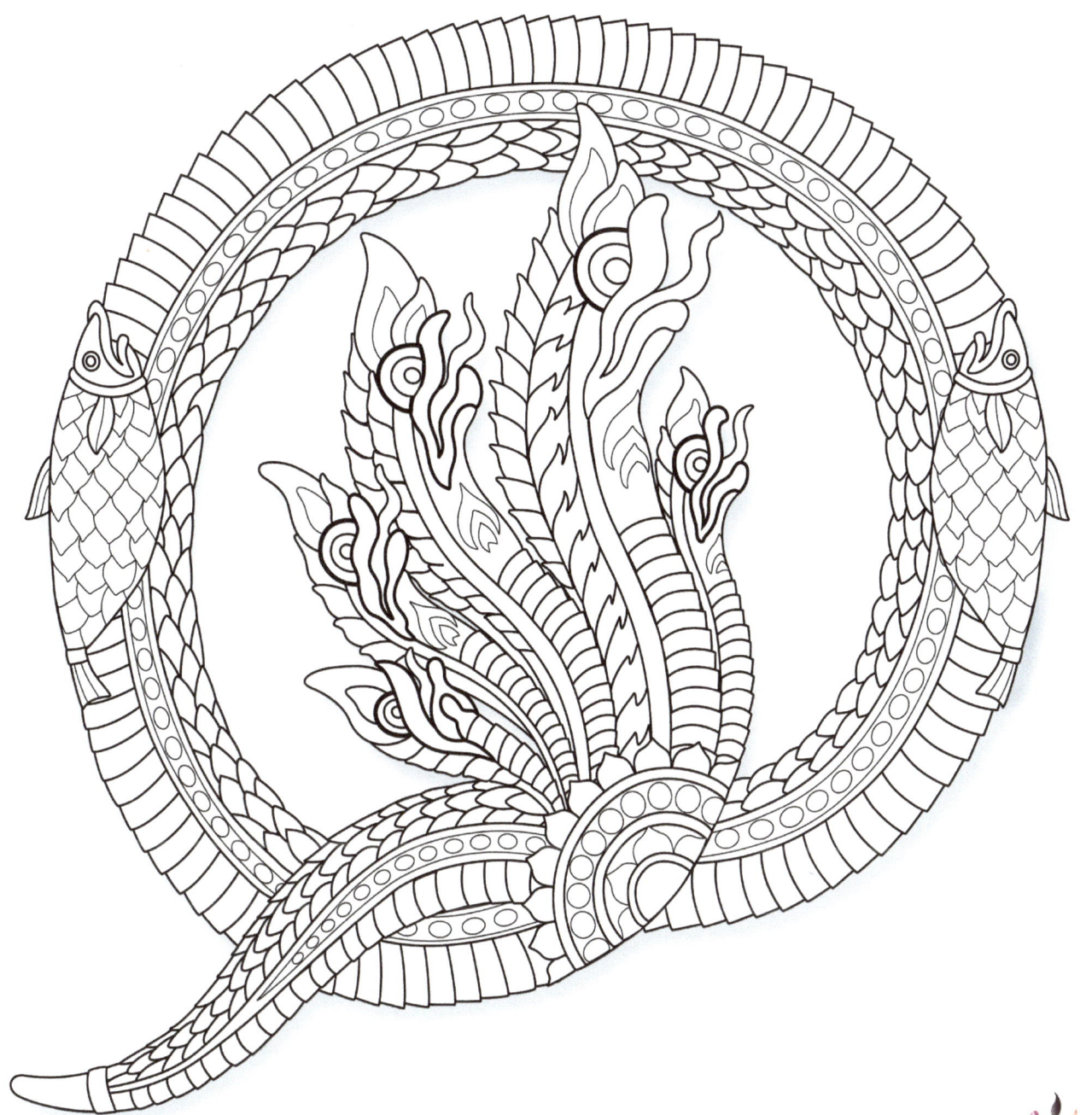

Color the drawing above using your preferred choice of colors.

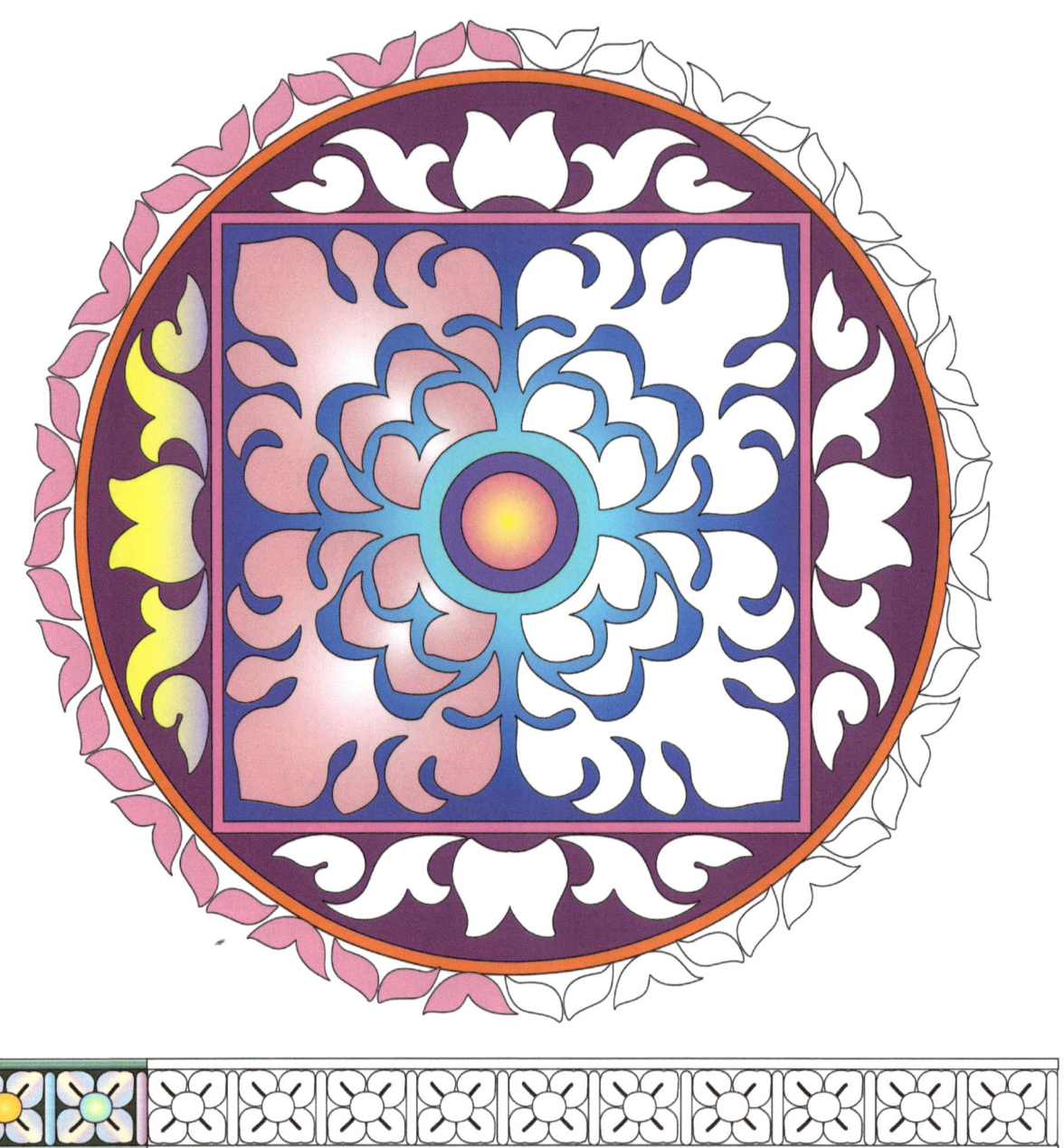

Color these images and create your own piece using the elements found in Cambodian Art.

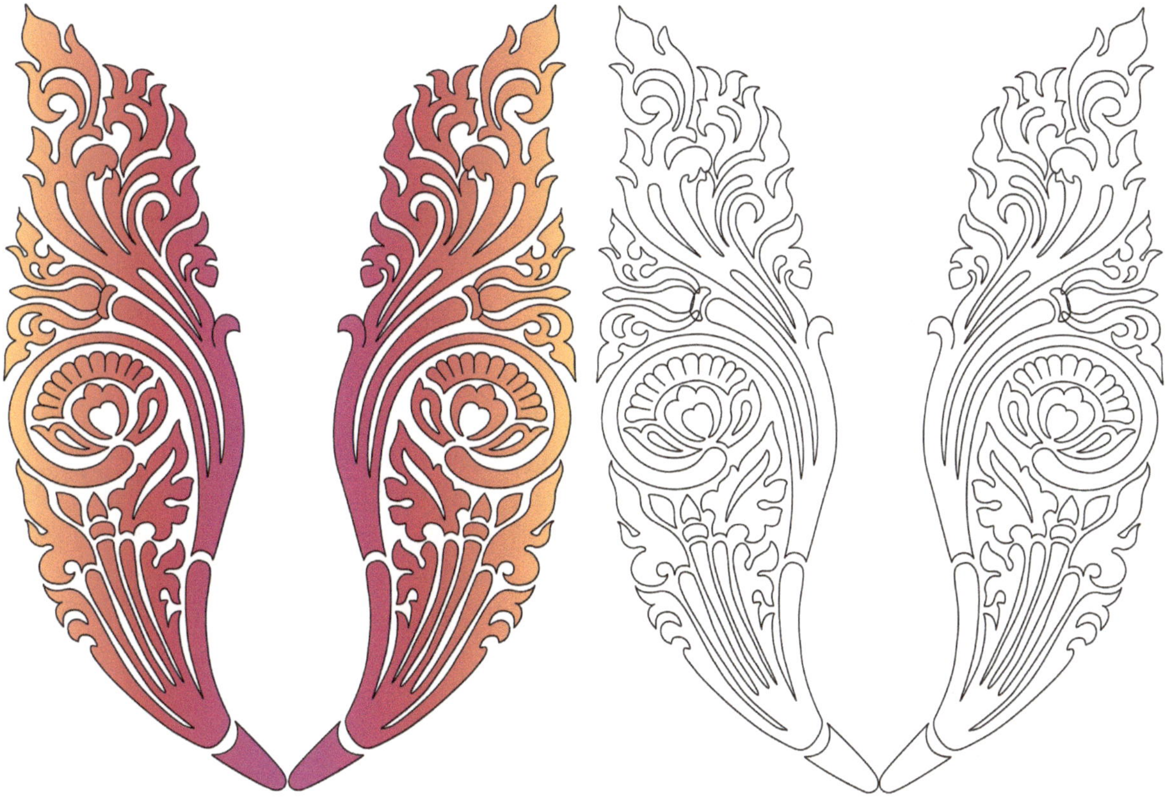

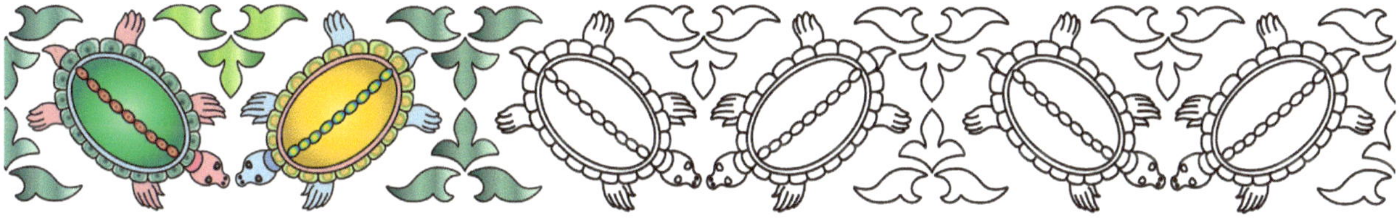

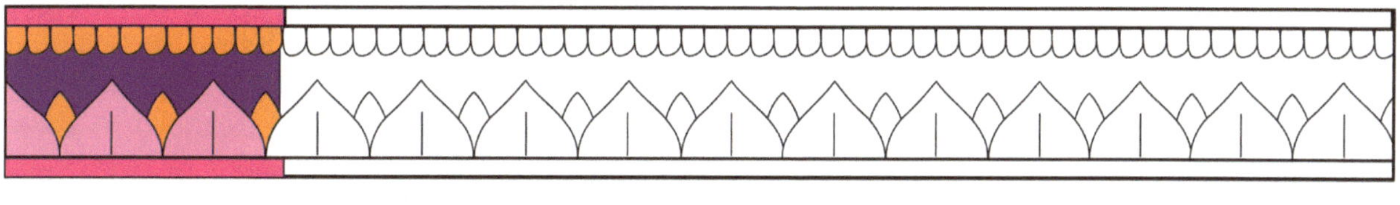

Color these images and create your own piece using the elements found in Cambodian Art.

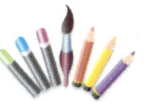

= a synopsis of =
Camb⬤dian art

Khmer art reached its peak during the Angkor period, and between 900 and 1200 C.E., the Khmer Empire was some of the world's most magnificent architectural beauty. The word Angkor derived from the Sanskrit word Nagar, which means city. The formidably enormous and incomparable monuments, the greatness along with beauty, and the vast wealth and strength of the Angkorian Civilization lasted some five centuries. Angkor was built especially for the divine powers of the Kings of Angkor.

Cambodian art stretches far back to the centuries old potteries, silk weaving, and stone carvings. Stone carving in Cambodia is the best-known form of art. They adorned the temples at Angkor and are renowned for their scale, richness, and the fine details of the sculptures. Cambodia's lacquer-ware were at its prime between the 12th and 16th Century C.E. Lacquer-ware were by tradition colored black using burnt wood to represent the underworld, red using mercury which symbolized the earth and yellow using arsenic to signify the heavens.

King Suryavarman II, who reigned over the Khmer Empire during 1113 - 1150 C.E., built the Angkor temples. Angkor Wat was the largest and the most harmonious of all the temples during that time. It was built within the period of 37 years and was solely dedicated to the God Vishnu. The temple represents the prodigious funeral pyre of a divine king, with its many towers, courtyards, and scenes from the great Indian epics, the Ramayana and the Mahabharata. In the Banteay Srei district, The Citadel of Women is the most popular and the style is even similar to the Indian style.

Years later, King Jayavarman VII, built the Bayon temple, which was his greatest undertaking in the centre of Angkor Thom. It is known to be the most extraordinary and yet strange monument in the world. The enormous sculpture is of a lotus with four faces, and eight eyes, multiplied by all the flowers appearing to envelop the whole world. They carved their lives, their laughter, their death, alongside the great friezes of the wars and triumphs with their warriors in chariots, and nobles in palanquins. They also carved various events from their domestic lives.

Unfortunately, later in the years, the Angkor Wat was left abandoned as the capital city of Khmers when the invaders settled in. Only in the early 20th Century was the city restored when a French explorer rediscovered it.

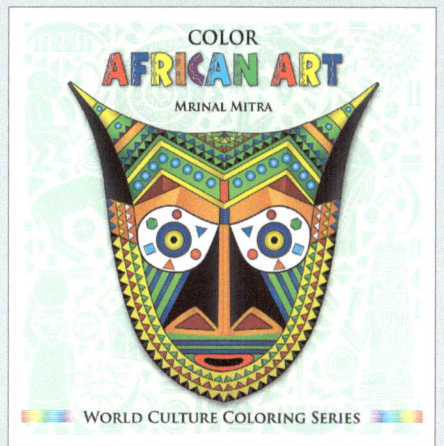

COLOR
AFRICAN ART
MRINAL MITRA
WORLD CULTURE COLORING SERIES

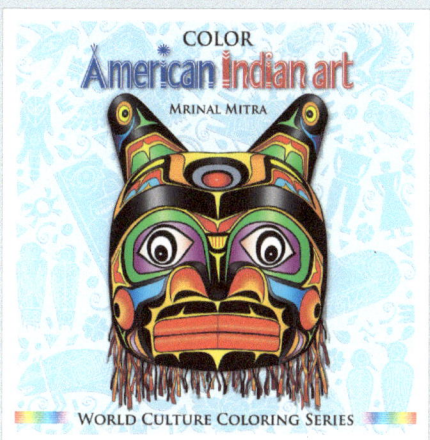

COLOR
American Indian art
MRINAL MITRA
WORLD CULTURE COLORING SERIES

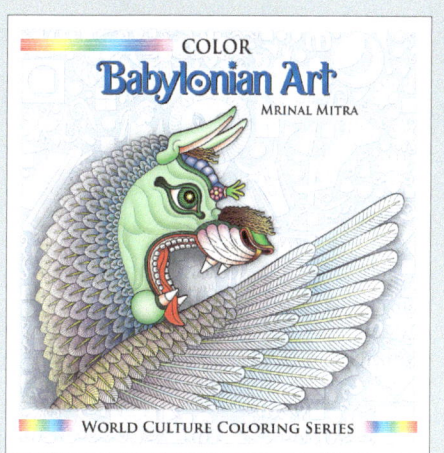

COLOR
Babylonian Art
MRINAL MITRA
WORLD CULTURE COLORING SERIES

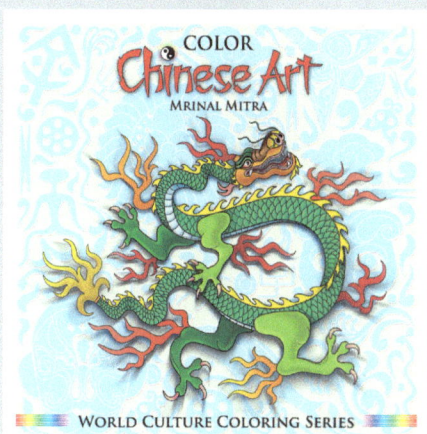

COLOR
Chinese Art
MRINAL MITRA
WORLD CULTURE COLORING SERIES

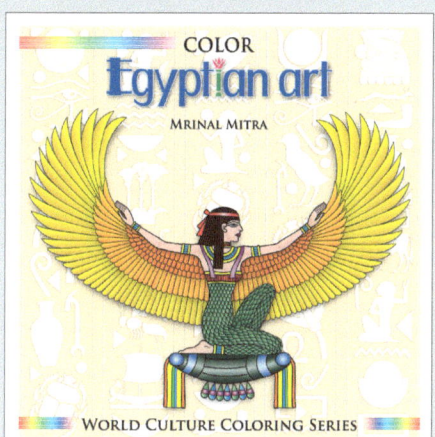

COLOR
Egyptian art
MRINAL MITRA
WORLD CULTURE COLORING SERIES

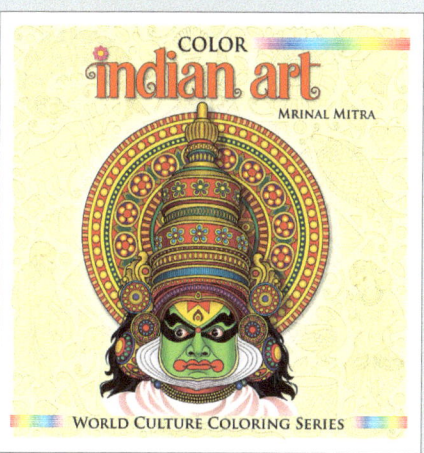

COLOR
indian art
MRINAL MITRA
WORLD CULTURE COLORING SERIES

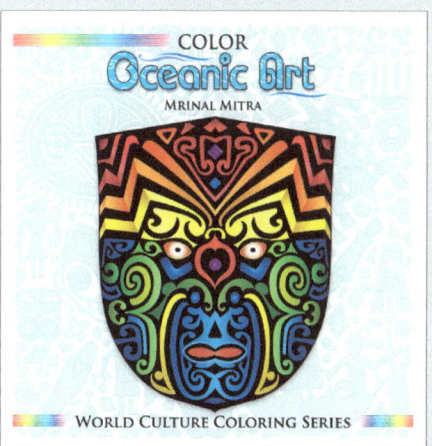

COLOR
Oceanic Art
MRINAL MITRA
WORLD CULTURE COLORING SERIES

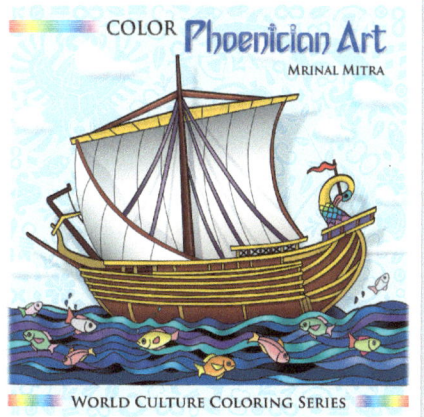

COLOR
Phoenician Art
MRINAL MITRA
WORLD CULTURE COLORING SERIES

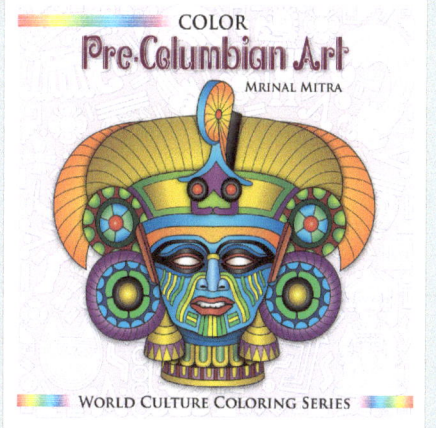

COLOR
Pre-Columbian Art
MRINAL MITRA
WORLD CULTURE COLORING SERIES

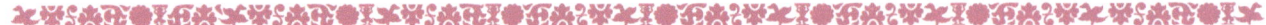

Acknowledgement

First and foremost, this series would not be possible without the number of great historical art found within the different cultural regions around the world.

In addition, we would like to acknowledge the variety of publishing's from all over the world for allowing us to learn about their fascinating ancestral art and culture. With this provided knowledge, we have hoped to have represented the art as splendidly as you have supplied it.

About the Author

Mrinal Mitra has earned a number of prestigious awards, both Indian and International, and received honors for his outstanding illustrations. Some of his recognitions include; The Noma Concours Award, Japan (twice), Illustrators Award, and Children's Choice Award, India, and honors from German Television "Transtel", BRNO- CSSR, TIBI- Iran, and UNICEF, New York.

Many of his talented artworks have been exhibited in several different countries such as; India, Japan, Italy, Czech Republic, Iran, and New Zealand. Mitra has authored, designed and illustrated trade and educational children's books for many Indian as well as Multinational Book Publishers around the globe.

Copyright: Mrinal Mitra, 2014

Printed by CreateSpace, An Amazon.com. Company
Available from Amazon.com, CreateSpace.com, and other retail outlets

For further inquiry please contact Mrinal Mitra at: mitra_mrinal@hotmail.com

www.ingramcontent.com/pod-product-compliance
Lightning Source LLC
Chambersburg PA
CBHW050840180526
45159CB00004B/1969